MW01015888

ABORIGINALITY

WITHDRAWN
FROM COLLECTION
VANCOUVER PUBLIC LIBRARY

OTHER BOOKS BY ALAN TWIGG

First Invaders: The Literary Origins of British Columbia
(Ronsdale Press, 2004)
101 Top Historical Sites of Cuba (Beach Holme Publishing, 2004)
Intensive Care: A Memoir (Anvil Press, 2002)
Cuba: A Concise History for Travelers
(Bluefield Books, 2000; Penguin Books, 2002; Harbour, 2005)
Twigg's Directory of 1001 BC Writers (Crown Publications, 1992)
Strong Voices: Conversations with 50 Canadian Writers (Harbour, 1988)
Vander Zalm, From Immigrant to Premier (Harbour, 1986)
Vancouver and Its Writers (Harbour, 1986)
Hubert Evans: The First Ninety-Three Years (Harbour, 1985)
For Openers: Conversations with 24 Canadian Writers (Harbour, 1981)

ABORIGINALITY

The Literary Origins of British Columbia, Vol. 2

ALAN TWIGG

RONSDALE

ABORIGINALITY
Copyright © 2005 Alan Twigg

All rights reserved. No part of this publication may be reproduced, stored in a retrieval system, or transmitted, in any form or by any means, without prior written permission of the publisher, or, in Canada, in the case of photocopying or other reprographic copying, a license from Access Copyright (the Canadian Copyright Licensing Agency).

RONSDALE PRESS
3350 West 21st Avenue
Vancouver, B.C., Canada V6S 1G7
www.ronsdalepress.com

Typesetting: Get To The Point Graphics, in New Baskerville 11 pt on 14.1
Cover Image: Pauline Johnson's favourite image of herself,
    courtesy of Simon Fraser University Special Collections
Back Cover Image: Penticton, B.C., 1995
Cover Design: David Lester
Paper: Ancient Forest Friendly Rolland "Enviro" – 100% post-consumer
    waste, totally chlorine-free and acid-free

Ronsdale Press wishes to thank the Canada Council for the Arts, the Government of Canada through the Book Publishing Industry Development Program (BPIDP), and the Province of British Columbia through the British Columbia Arts Council for their support of its publishing program.

Library and Archives Canada Cataloguing in Publication

Twigg, Alan, 1952-
Aboriginality: the literary origins of British Columbia / Alan Twigg.

Includes bibliographical references and index.
ISBN 1-55380-030-3

1. Native peoples in literature. 2. Canadian literature (English) — Native authors —Biography. 3. Authors, Canadian (English)— British Columbia—Biography. 4. Native peoples — British Columbia. I. Title. II. Title: Literary origins of British Columbia.

PS8089.5.I6T84 2005   C810.9'352997   C2005-903526-9

At Ronsdale Press we are committed to protecting the environment. To this end we are working with Markets Initiative (www.oldgrowthfree.com) and printers to phase out our use of paper produced from ancient forests. This book is one step towards that goal.

Printed in Canada by Marquis

To the unheralded

and to George & Ingeborg,
gone but not forgotten.

NOV 2 9 2005

Skyros Bruce, at age twenty, published the first book of poetry written entirely by an Aboriginal woman born in British Columbia.

KOA S 2 3002

CONTENTS

ACKNOWLEDGEMENTS

Once more I am primarily indebted to David Lester for his collaboration as a designer and friend. Particular thanks must also go to photographers Barry Peterson and Vickie Jensen for their numerous portraits. I have especially benefited from the generous responses of Vickie and her husband Jay Powell, one of the province's most constructive anthropologists and linguists–two neighbours who became friends.

Numerous photographs are from the *BC BookWorld* archives, or were taken during my travels. For other photographs and research materials, I wish to acknowledge the ongoing partnership of B.C. publishers and authors, Simon Fraser University Special Collections (Eric Swanick, Tony Power), Macleod's Books (Don Stewart), UBC Special Collections (Ralph Stanton), Vancouver Public Library (Paul Whitney), City of Vancouver Archives, *Encyclopedia of British Columbia*, Mission Community Archives, Chilliwack Museum and Archives, Yale Museum and Archives (Bruce Mason), and Merritt Museum and Archives.

"Cy Pitt" by Arthur Twigg, 1985

I am also grateful to editor/publisher Ronald Hatch, who tells the truth and does things on time, as well as Fernanda Viveiros and Catherine Whitehead at Ronsdale Press, my agent Don Sedgwick, booksellers Don Stewart and David W. Ellis, Madeline MacIvor at the First Nations House of Learning, UBC Press editor Jean Wilson and my sons Jeremy and Martin for their research and patience.

Finally, writing this book has made me appreciate the many paintings and drawings undertaken by my late father to express his lifelong affinity for indigenous culture.

— A.T.

FOREWORD

*"The government of Canada only understands
the 26 letters of the alphabet."*
— GARRY GOTTFRIEDSON,
SECWEPEMC POET AND HORSE BREEDER

When Garry Gottfriedson made his remark in Salmon Arm, he was explaining the integral roles his parents had played as activists in the movement that resulted in the ascendancy of their Shuswap leader George Manuel. I jotted it down without thinking. It had a ring to it.

Now it serves as a succinct explanation as to why this book exists. As Gottfriedson realized, in Canada we fight mostly with words. In that context, the growing English language proficiency of First Nations people—and their ability to persuasively use those "26 letters of the alphabet" on paper—has generated a literary movement of immense importance.

In British Columbia, where the country's first Aboriginal-owned and -operated publishing company was founded in 1980, the recent proliferation of books for, by and about Aboriginals—the term used in the Canadian constitution to designate "Indians," Inuit and Métis—merits documentation and celebration.

Aboriginality, volume two of "The Literary Origins of British Columbia," introduces more than 170 Aboriginal authors (including painters, carvers, illustrators and editors) who have produced three hundred books since 1900.

These authors are arranged mainly chronologically, in terms of their first pub-

Garry Gottfriedson

lished works, rather than alphabetically or in accordance with tribal origins (often mixed), geography or literary genres (often mixed). This approach allows for easy appreciation of changing themes as well as the surge of literary activity that was spurred by the appearance of a viable B.C. publishing industry in general, and the establishment of Theytus Books, founded by Randy Fred, and the En'owkin Centre, overseen by Jeannette C. Armstrong, in particular.

In our newspapers we frequently learn about the hardwon progress made by Aboriginals through our legal system, and we have recently benefited from a surge of more than one thousand British Columbia-related books pertaining to "Indianology"— the study and marketing of First Nations culture—but the

uprising of literature from Aboriginals in B.C. has seldom been celebrated or even cited.

Aboriginality is the first attempt in book format to identify the books by First Nations peoples in B.C. or, for that matter, in any Canadian province. I hope this assembly of biographical, cultural and bibliographical information amounts to cultural news.

⸺⸺⟨∘∘∘⟩⸺⸺

I have limited my definition of literature herein to books. Others are welcome to expand their definition to include oral storytelling and petroglyphs (both subjects for many books already.) A separate entry is accorded to each author. As *Aboriginality* is intended to introduce a wide spectrum of (mostly) hitherto unknown Aboriginal writers, it seemed important not to subdue individual writers and their books to any overarching theme.

As with the first volume in this series, an extensive bibliography is provided. There is also an index of authors. To the alarm of one reviewer, extracts of volume one (and now volume two) can be easily copied (at www.abcbookworld.com). My goal is to disseminate useful information. Most people know precious little about the literary history of British Columbia and I have always preferred to write for most people.

———✦———

A word on terminology: in a province where the majority of people are from somewhere else, and change is coming quickly to many Aboriginal communities, it is difficult to get everyone on the same page about specific names used to describe First Nations people and places. Haida Gwaii and the Queen Charlotte Islands have become interchangeable terms. Do you prefer Interior Salish, Thompson Indians, Niakapmux or 'Nlaka'pamux? Should we write Gitksan, Gitxsan or Gitxsan?

I am not a schoolteacher whose job it is to change the spelling of others, or a geographer with the power to alter the world atlas. This book was written in English, not Haida or Kwak'wala. Nevertheless, in a place where nearly everyone has learned to pronounce Tsawwassen with a silent T, I hope we can continue to embrace linguistic diversity. I leave the literary policing to others.

It should also be noted that writing in English by Canada's Aboriginal peoples, who favoured an oral culture for millennia, is a relatively new phenomenon. Less than one hundred years ago, most tribes in British Columbia were dependent on the services of intermediaries such as James Teit, the conciliatory Peter Kelly (who supported the government ban of the potlatch), or white missionaries, to represent their viewpoints in print.

A reluctance by Aboriginal communities to adopt English was understandable. Obviously one way to preserve indigenous culture was *not* to conform to the dictates of so-called white society. Hence literacy in English was seen as a double-edged sword: it gave individuals greater resources within the mainstream society, but literate Aboriginals were more prone to leave the reserves and thus lose their traditional values and way of life.

As well, those Aboriginals who are willing to credit the deservedly maligned residential school system for teaching them how to read and write the English language tend to do so quietly. Memories of residential schools cut deep. In a nutshell, the learning of English has been connected to cruelty for generations. Hence the advent of published Aboriginal authors in British Columbia as a new "norm" in our society represents a painful triumph of both will and endurance.

To this day, Aboriginals who earn university degrees are sometimes not fully trusted within their own tribes. Arguably, they have "gone over to the side." In some cases, they are even discriminated against.

For earlier Aboriginals, the English language has been a burden and a curse to be overcome, slowly, and with caution, rather than a system of communication that could be taken for granted. One early example concerning events arising from the so-called Chilcotin War illustrates this fear of the written word.

Once upon a darker time, when the written word was used as a tool of oppression, the Reverend R.C. Lundin Brown, a clergyman at St. Mary's Parsonage in Lillooet from 1863 to 1865, described his efforts to convert six Tsilhqot'in (Chilcotin) men who were sentenced to hang by Judge Matthew Begbie in the aftermath of violence in April of 1864. While defending their territory near Bute Inlet against the incursion of road builders who had verbally threatened them with the advent of a smallpox epidemic if they did not cooperate, the Tsilhqot'in had killed 14 intruders.

The Reverend Brown wrote: "They have, be it observed, a very special horror of having their names written down. They look upon paper as a very awful thing, they tremble to see the working of a pen. Writing is, they imagine, a dread mystery. By it the mighty whites seem to carry on intercourse with unseen powers.

"When they are writing, there's no telling what they may be doing. They may be bidding a pestilence come over the land, or ordering the rain to stay in the west, or giving directions for the salmon to remain in the ocean.

"Especially is the Indian appalled when he sees his own name put on paper. To him the name is not distinct from the person who owns it. If his name is written down, he is written down: if his name is passed over to the demons which people his hierarchy, he is sure to be bewitched and given as prey into the teeth of his invisible foes.

"So when those Chilcoatens [sic] saw their names taken down and heard themselves threatened with disease, they were only too ready to believe the threat. . . . Had not the Shuschwaps [sic] lost many of their warriors? and the Indians who lived away at Lillooet, on the great river, as many as two-thirds of their whole tribe?

"It was only too likely that those awful whites would fulfill their threat, and send the foulest of all diseases which ever came forth from the jaws of hell, to sweep their tribes away into everlasting night." So in the beginning was the Word—as well as guns, Bibles, booze and disease.

———

Whereas the literary activity charted in *Aboriginality* spans approximately a century, the backdrop for Aboriginal storytelling stretches back at least ten thousand years. Some acknowledgement of that expansive cultural legacy, from which a new literary culture has only recently emerged, seems necessary.

The oldest known site of human habitation in British Columbia, the Charlie Lake Cave near Fort St. John, contains tools, bison bones and jewellery, radio carbon-dated to 10,500 years ago. The oldest skeletal remains belong to a young male caught in a mudslide at Gore Creek, east of Kamloops, approximately 8,300 years ago. These bones were recently repatriated for interment in Secwepemc territory.

One of the largest prehistoric village sites in Western Canada is at Keatley Creek, about 20 kilometres upstream from Lillooet, where approximately fifteen hundred people resided in more than one hundred houses between ten and twenty centuries ago.

And then came the newcomers. The first verifiable meeting between Aboriginals and Europeans within what is now B.C. ter-

Bird amulet collected by Juan Pérez in 1774

ritory occurred near Langara Island, at the north end of the Queen Charlotte Islands, on July 19, 1774. Three canoes approached the Spanish ship *Santiago* under the command of Juan Pérez at around 4:30 in the afternoon. Captain Pérez, his second-in-command Esteban José Martínez and two Catholic priests recorded the meeting in their journals.

One of the Spanish officers tossed a biscuit, wrapped in a kerchief, into one of the canoes. Eager to barter, and having learned the value of metal from Russians to the north, the tribe (likely Haida) traded fish for beads and returned the following day, about one hundred of them, in more than a dozen canoes.

That day Juan Pérez acquired a painted bird amulet, to be worn around the neck, "with a string of teeth that appeared to be those of a baby alligator." Made from a whale's tooth, this carved amulet—one of the oldest artefacts from B.C.—is on display at the Museõ de America in Madrid.

Among the items acquired by Aboriginals during Pérez's two known anchorages—the other near the entrance to Nootka Sound—were two Spanish spoons. These two eating utensils ("evidently not English make") resurfaced as significant trade items in 1778 when Captain Cook arrived at Nootka Sound with his subordinates William Bligh and George Vancouver. The purchase of the two spoons by a British seaman aboard the *Resolution*—as recorded in four British memoirs of the voyage—was later cited by the Spanish to prove

Eagle mask collected during Captain James Cook's visit to Nootka Sound in 1778

the British were not the first Europeans to reach British Columbia.

The complicated relationships between Chief Maquinna's people at Nootka Sound and the flurry of British, Spanish, French and American mariners in the late eighteenth century have been recalled in *First Invaders: The Literary Origins of British Columbia*, the predecessor to this volume.

George Clutesi was bequeathed the brushes of Emily Carr.

Since the arrivals of Pérez and Cook in the late eighteenth century, Aboriginals have had minimal impact on the process of formally recording British Columbia history on paper.

For most of the twentieth century, the best-known Aboriginal authors were celebrated as Indians first, writers second. Pauline Johnson was a theatrical recitalist who lived in Vancouver for only four years. Chief Dan George was primarily an actor. George Clutesi was regarded as a painter, actor and broadcaster.

Prior to the 1980s, most books credited to Aboriginal authors were of the "as told to" variety. As *Aboriginality* reveals, a surge of literary activity began as Aboriginals themselves learned to take control of the means of production. An urbane uprising of self-confidence occurred. This change is reflected in the contents of *Aboriginality*.

From the early 1980s onward, the literary climate for Aboriginals in British Columbia has been changing rapidly, prompted by Aboriginal publishing and the nurturing of writers at the En'owkin Centre in Penticton. Accordingly, "Voices from the Wilderness," the opening section of this book, concludes with the establishment of Theytus Books in 1981, leading to "Seeing Red," marked by the publication of Jeannette Armstrong's first book. A third section entitled "Artists and Carvers" includes individuals not primarily known for their literary activities, followed by 55 condensed entries for "Also Noteworthy." The bibliography is restricted to titles written or illustrated by Aboriginals.

———————

My father grew up in West Vancouver with Indian friends, but gradually these family friendships disappeared until a virtual apartheid ensued.

I learned to say a few words of Chinook and I wore Cowichan Indian sweaters to school, but my contact with the Aboriginal community in West Vancouver was restricted to rare soccer games on the Capilano Indian Reserve where their pitch was bumpy, their players were athletic but disorganized, and the games were rough. There was never any fraternization afterwards beyond a grudging handshake.

Since then we have been making some hard-won progress. As a society, we are collectively making some amends; we are slowly getting reacquainted.

Aboriginal people currently comprise approximately 4.4 percent of the B.C. population according to a StatsCan 2001 survey, but their distinct histories and their imaginative universes can have enormous significance for anyone who can look beyond their television set.

As a fifth-generation Vancouverite, I want to understand better how Aboriginal societies are integral to where I live. A follow-up volume is being prepared to address the remarkable range of more than one thousand titles pertaining to B.C.'s First Nations and written by non-Aboriginals, but it struck me as appropriate to present first the emerging field of B.C. Aboriginal writing, a hitherto unmarked literary zone

Most tribes did not sign treaties in B.C. They did not legally relinquish their territories. Therefore all British Columbians are challenged by a morally perplexing history. If we have inherited social problems, they need to be fixed. Cumulatively the pain and poverty, the prejudice and persecutions of the past cannot be expunged, but at least the past can be fully acknowledged.

The notion that the Aboriginal peoples of this province are the original peoples of this province with distinct societies, and that they deserve to be "citizens plus" (to borrow a term from Alan C. Cairns and Harold Cardinal) because they were "citizens minus" for so long, still appears seditious to some people. And yet progress at reconciliation is being made, even among those for whom the "nation-to-nation paradigm" is problematic.

Some 72 percent of British Columbia's Aboriginals are now living in urban environments, not on Reserves. According to Madeline MacIvor of the First Nations House of Learning at UBC, a significant portion of these are leaders in the struggle to redefine the place of the Aboriginal community in Canada. Within that process, British Columbia leads the way in Aboriginal literature.

In the words of carver and photographer David Neel, "Today we are witnessing the rebirth of our cultures on the Northwest Coast. We can see the end of a period of oppression, and we can see a time of hope for our grandchildren. We are entering into a time in which Aboriginal people have a place in contemporary society. The Native has learned much; it is now time that society learn from the Native."

Publisher G.S. Forsythe sold Legends of Vancouver *by E. Pauline Johnson from his bookstore at 349 West Hastings (circa 1913).*

I
VOICES FROM THE WILDERNESS

BC ARCHIVES PHOTO # A-02198

Also a lacemaker and painter, British Columbia's first female Métis author, Martha Douglas Harris, was wed in 1878, one year after her famous father's death.

ABORIGINALITY

MARTHA DOUGLAS HARRIS

Emily Pauline Johnson is generally acknowledged as the starting point for Aboriginal writing in British Columbia, but she was actually the second Aboriginal woman to publish from the West Coast. The first was the youngest daughter of the most powerful figure in British Columbia during the nineteenth century, Sir James Douglas.

Despite her father's objections, the multi-talented Martha Douglas Harris (1854-1933) published *History and Folklore of the Cowichan Indians* (1901), the first commercial compilation of Aboriginal stories from and about the province, predating Pauline Johnson's *Legends of Vancouver* by ten years.

As the founder of Fort Victoria and the second governor of Vancouver Island, Sir James Douglas was wary of how much his daughter's book revealed about their family's background. Born in British Guiana in 1803 as the son of a Creole mother and a Scottish-born merchant, he was not chiefly concerned about his own black ancestry.

Douglas was sensitive about the fact that his wife, Lady Amelia Douglas, was born in 1812 at Fort Assiniboine, the daughter of fur trader William Connolly and his Cree wife Miyo Nipiy. "I have no objection to your telling the old stories about Hyas," he wrote to his daughter, when Martha Douglas was taking classes for elocution, drawing, French, composition and music in England, "but pray do not tell the world they are Mamma's."

Partially based on stories told to her by her half-Cree mother, Harris' compilation of 14 Cowichan and six Cree stories did eventually include "The Adventures of Hyas" as its concluding story. It is a stirring tale of supernatural events and murderous revenge in which an unfairly banished son, stranded on an island by his

21

cruel father, ultimately returns to rescue his mother.

Having undergone various ordeals in the wilderness, Hyas instructs his mother to burn alive his wicked stepmother's infant. After everyone else in his father's village is drowned, Hyas transforms himself into a red-breasted bird and transforms his mother into a lark.

The giantess Zoohalitz (above, from History & Folklore of the Cowichan Indians*) "snatched up the poor fellow in her arms and smothered him with her foul breath and kisses."*

Printed in Victoria, Harris' book was illustrated by her friend Margaret C. Maclure, wife of architect Samuel Maclure. Although the stories lack anthropological or literary merit, they are dignified second-hand renditions, seemingly without artifice.

"When written down," Harris admitted of her stories, "they lose their charm which was in the telling. They need the quaint songs and the sweet voice that told them, the winter loaming and the bright fire as the only light—then were these legends beautiful."

Martha Harris' respect for First Nations culture was not merely romantic. She gathered a collection of Aboriginal basketry that is now housed at the Royal British Columbia Museum and she maintained friendships with Aboriginal families living on the Songhees Reserve on the edge of Victoria.

In 1912, in response to the relocation of the Songhees people to Esquimalt, following the government's purchase of the valuable Songhees Reserve lands, Harris expressed her dismay and consternation in a letter to the editor of the *Daily Colonist.* Harris described the plight of her friend Tom James, a Cowichan who had married a Songhees woman.

"If by law a white man acquired land by adverse possession of 12 or 20 years," she argued, "why has Tom James not acquired an equally good right by 34 years' undisputed possession? . . . Must the government conjure up technicalities to find an excuse for depriving this man and his wife of their equitable claim?"

The youngest of six children, Martha Douglas married colonial official Dennis Harris in a lavish wedding in 1878. Having learned to add native plant dyes to wool, Harris taught other women how to weave and encouraged the local production of spinning wheels in Victoria. Her own spinning wheel was donated to Helmcken House in the 1930s.

E. PAULINE JOHNSON

The only literary monument erected in Vancouver for a Canadian writer during the twentieth century—the Pauline Johnson memorial in Stanley Park, above Third Beach—commemorates the Mohawk princess who specifically requested in her will that no such memorial be built.

Emily Pauline Johnson was born near Brantford, Ontario, on March 10, 1861. As the youngest of four children, she lived at the Chiefswood mansion on the eastern bank of the Grand River, at the edge of the Grand River Reservation, on a 200-acre estate, until age twenty-two.

Her father, Chief George Henry Martin Johnson, the son of a half-white mother, Helen Martin, was the church translator prior to his marriage in 1853. A Chief of the Six Nations who was fluent in several languages, he taught his daughter how to use a canoe, a skill that would result in her best-known poem, "The Song My Paddle Sings" ("Be strong, O paddle! be brave, canoe!"). She was also greatly influenced by her grandfather John Smoke Johnson (1792–1885).

Pauline Johnson's mother was Emily Susanna (Howells), sister-in-law of Reverend Adam Elliot, the Anglican missionary for the reserve. As a member of a relatively free-thinking family that included Quaker abolitionists, she kindled her daughter's interest in English Romantic poetry.

Pauline Johnson as she appeared before Queen Victoria in London, England, in 1906

At age fourteen, Pauline Johnson was enrolled in the Brantford Collegiate Institute but she left that school in 1877. The relatively well-to-do Johnson clan encouraged assimilation with the Euro-Canadian society as Christians, but also struggled to maintain cultural ties with the increasingly splintered Six Nations community.

Pauline Johnson's father died in 1884 after he was beaten by white liquor traders who resented his efforts to impede their commerce among his people. At age twenty-two, Johnson, her mother and her sister Evelyn were forced to move to much more modest accommodations in Brantford. She would publish some 60 poems in North American periodicals, including *Saturday Night* magazine and *The Week* magazine, during the next seven years, branching into prose in 1890. While at Brantford she published her first poem in *Gems of Poetry* (New York) in 1885.

Johnson's career as an entertainer was launched in January of 1892 when she was invited by Frank Yeigh to address the Young Liberal Club of Toronto during a Canadian Literary Evening. Her recitation of "A Cry from an Indian Wife," previously published by *The Week* in 1885, proved sufficiently popular for her to design a memorable stage costume in the autumn of 1892. To reinforce her new-found theatrical reputation as the Mohawk Princess, she created an asymmetrical buckskin dress adorned with various regalia that later included a necklace of bear claws given to her by the naturalist author Ernest Thompson Seton. This "get-up" of silver brooches, wampum belts, her father's hunting knife and a scalp given to her by a Blackfoot chief was partially inspired by an artist's rendering of the character of Minnehaha from Longfellow's poem about Hiawatha.

At age thirty, Johnson began her theatrical career as a poet-entertainer, mirroring her duality by performing the first half of her program in her Indian regalia, and the second half in an evening dress. She also adopted the Aboriginal name of her great-grandfather Jacob Johnson, a hero of the War of 1812, as her stage name. Tekahionwake, meaning Double Wampum, referred to the strung-together white and purple Atlantic shells that were used as currency by her Aboriginal ancestors.

In 1892, Johnson began touring Ontario with Owen Smiley, the first of several male co-performers, honing her performances in the north-eastern United States before crossing the Atlantic for the first time in 1894. Carrying letters of introduction from Lord and Lady Aberdeen, she entertained British audiences and was introduced by Canadian novelist Sir Gilbert Parker to John Lane, publisher of risqué authors Aubrey Beardsley and Oscar Wilde. Lane was sufficiently impressed by the exotic colonial to issue her first poetry collection *The White Wampum* (1895) from the Bodley Head. Although less than one-quarter of the text addressed First Nations topics, the front cover credited the author only as Tekahionwake and the artwork emphasized her Aboriginal heritage.

After her mother died in 1898, Johnson moved to Winnipeg where she became engaged to Charles Robert Lumley Drayton in 1898–1899 until the arrangement was mysteriously cancelled. Having visited British Columbia in 1894, she toured the Atlantic provinces in 1900. She became connected romantically with her manager, Charles Wuerz, but the exact nature of their relationship remains unknown. Thereafter Johnson toured extensively with her much younger stage partner, Walter McRaye, who remained by her side until 1909. One of her anonymous poems entitled "Both Sides" suggests the poignant incompatibility of their ages. It was necessary for Johnson to avoid scandal in order to continue to advertise herself as a well-mannered savage capable of behaving as a lady in drawing room society.

Returning to England, Johnson did much to cultivate a romanticized notion of her homeland and Aboriginal culture, simultaneously developing an ideal of Canadian nationalism in partnership with Great Britain, as evidenced by her stirring, patriotic poems such as "Canadian Born." In the preface to her second book of poetry, *Canadian Born* (1903), she optimistically proclaimed, "White Race and Red are one if they are but Canadian born."

Also visiting London in 1906, lobbying King Edward VI for

recognition of his people's land claims, was Chief Joe Capilano of Vancouver, with whom Johnson became a close friend. In her poem "Little Vancouver" that was inspired by her first visit in September of 1894, Johnson had already begun to champion the potential of the West Coast city to one day supplant Toronto. The willingness of Chief Capilano and his Squamish people to welcome her as a cultural hero furthered her affinity.

Pauline Johnson as a young woman

When visiting the West Coast, Johnson usually stayed at the Hotel Vancouver. Increasingly troubled by ill health, she announced her intention to live permanently in Vancouver in 1909 before an appreciative audience at the Pender Auditorium. Eschewing her career as a pop star of her times, she took an apartment at 1117 Howe Street and concentrated on her writing.

During the final ten years of her life Johnson published only 20 poems, increasingly turning her hand to essays and short fiction such as "The Potlatch" and "The Siwash Rock," her rendition of an Aboriginal story told by Chief Capilano. In 1910 she began publishing prose pieces in the *Saturday Province Magazine*, edited by Lionel Maskovski, and these were privately printed as a fundraising initiative on her behalf by the Pauline Johnson Trust Fund. This project proved to be a runaway bestseller, released in official and pirated editions, even after it was formally published as *Legends of Vancouver* (1911). A follow-up volume of selected poems called *Flint and Feather* (1912), combining poetry from her first two books, has proven to be one of the most-reprinted poetry collections in Canadian history, rivaling the works of Robert Service.

Suffering from painful and inoperable breast cancer, Johnson expressed her desire to be buried in Stanley Park. Wary of setting precedents, civic authorities agreed to Johnson's request with the proviso that she be cremated. Nine days prior to her death on March 7, 1913, just three days before reaching age fifty-two, Pauline Johnson requested that no structure be raised in her memory. She added, "I particularly desire that neither my sister or brother wear black nor what is termed mourning for me, as I have always disliked such displays of personal feelings. I desire that no mourning notepaper or stationery be used by them."

Literally thousands of people lined Georgia Street to witness her funeral procession, easily one of the most galvanizing events in Vancouver history. To ensure all her debts were paid, two more prose collections, *The Moccasin Maker* (1903) and *The Shagganappi* (1913), were published after her death. The Women's Canadian Club began its campaign to erect a stone cairn for the ashes in 1914.

When the editor of the *Vancouver World* newspaper received a $225 share for the sales of *Legends of Vancouver* in 1915 from the poet's sister, he used the money to launch a subscription fund to buy a gun for the 29th battalion during World War I. After enormous public response, the necessary $1,000 was raised and the gun was delivered to the troops. On the gun barrel was inscribed the word, Tekahionwake.

Insufficient funds delayed construction of the Pauline Johnson monument project until 1922 when a modest fountain, designed by James McLeod Hurry, was built in the woods near Third Beach, not far from Siwash Rock. Initial response to the memorial was mixed. Johnson's right profile is depicted looking away from her beloved Siwash Rock and the face and braided hairstyle were not representative. Pauline Johnson's sister commented in 1924, "I do not like the way Vancouver seems to claim Pauline. Pauline lived all her life in the East with the exception of about four years which were passed in Vancouver where she died."

Domanic Charlie (left) and Chief Joe Mathias at the Pauline Johnson Memorial, 1961

A Vancouver chocolate company adopted Pauline Johnson's name for their product in the 1920s, thereby rivaling Laura Secord chocolates in Ontario, and William McRaye protected and advanced Pauline Johnson's literary reputation until his own death in 1946.

Neglected during World War II, the Pauline Johnson monument was stripped of its bronze by thieves in 1945. It was desecrated with red paint in 1953. *Vancouver Sun* book columnist Don Stainsby reported the dilapidated condition of the monument in 1961, the same year the Canadian government issued a commemorative stamp in March to mark the centenary of her birth. Like the depiction on her monument, the honorary stamp didn't bear much resemblance to Johnson. The Vancouver Parks Board refurbished the memorial in 1981, the same year novelist Ethel Wilson recorded her impressions of Johnson in "The Princess," an article printed in *Canadian Literature.*

Ethel Wilson never forgot meeting Johnson and acknowledged that she "pursued a path of her own making, and did this with integrity until the last day of her life." In this regard, although she was not an outspoken suffragist, Johnson strongly advocated outdoor exercise for women. While stressing the need to forge a separate Canadian identity, Johnson persevered for 30 years as an artist, remaining financially independent, unmarried and untouched by scandal.

While some have glorified Pauline Johnson as an independent female artist and an advocate for Aboriginal pride, the majority of her published writing was not about First Nations material, she never learned to speak an Aboriginal language and the quality of her writing has been less easy to celebrate than her reputation. Historian Daniel Francis suggested in *The Imaginary Indian: The Image of the Indian in Canadian Culture* (1992), the "need to satisfy the demands of a White audience stultified Pauline Johnson's development as a writer and limited her effectiveness as a spokesperson for Native people." In terms of literature, she is mostly remembered for her poems "The Song My Paddle Sings" and "The Legend of the Qu'Appelle," as well as her transformed versions of stories told to her by Chief Joe Capilano and Mary Capilano of the Squamish Indian Band. Pauline Johnson wanted their book to be called *Legends of the Capilanos* but for marketing reasons it was released as *Legends of Vancouver.*

JOE & MARY CAPILANO

Although Mary Capilano (Lixwelut) and Chief Joe Capilano (Su-a-pu-luck) are not cited as co-authors of Pauline Johnson's *Legends of Vancouver* (1911), they provided the basis for the stories that explain the origins of Siwash Rock and the twin peaks known as the Lions.

In addition to recalling how the first Chief Capilano wounded a giant seal in False Creek in 1820 and how he shot 13 elk from the last elk herd in Vancouver, taking the meat by canoe to Victoria for sale, the collection cites the chief's tribal knowledge of Napoleon Bonaparte that was gained from French captives of a Russian ship. Johnson praises Chief Capilano's halting English as "always quaint and beautiful."

Capilano was born near Squamish circa 1840 and lived mainly on the Catholic mission reserve near the Capilano River.

In 1889 he guided the first white party to make a recorded ascent of the West Lion mountain on the North Shore. A year later he led an expedition

Mary Capilano (right) waits for the Queen, 1939.

Chief Capilano met King Edward in London in 1906.

to the source of the Capilano River. He was known as a carver but worked as a sawmill labourer and stevedore, becoming chief in 1895.

In 1906, along with Cowichan Chief Charley Isipaymilt and Shuswap Chief Basil David, Capilano led a delegation to England, at his own expense, to meet King Edward VI and lobby for recognition of his people's land claims. His expedition was belittled in the local press when he left Vancouver but he succeeded in gaining access to the King and obtaining a sympathetic hearing. Upon his return, Capilano was labeled a troublemaker for repeating comments allegedly made by King Edward and for organizing a meeting of northern and southern tribes in 1907.

He died on March 11, 1910, in North Vancouver prior to publication of his "legends," as retold by Johnson. Those stories proved influential on his descendant Lee Maracle, a novelist and activist who first received a copy of *Legends of Vancouver* when she was ten or eleven. She recalls being particularly impressed by Capilano's retelling of the sea serpent story in which he predicts the industrialization of Canada.

Mary Agnes Capilano (1836?–1940) was an important genealogist and storyteller. Her grandfather met George Vancouver upon his arrival on June 13, 1792, in Burrard Inlet. She was the first-born daughter of Chief Skakhult whose marriage had united two previously warring tribes, the Yaculta and the Squamish.

In 1936, without consultation and little compensation, the Minister of Indian Affairs recommended transfer of lands from Capilano Indian Reserve No. 5 to the First Narrows Bridge Company, pursuant to Section 48 of the Indian Act. Three years later, when King George VI and Queen Elizabeth became the first English monarchs to visit Canada, they drove over the Lions Gate Bridge to "honour it."

The Squamish requested the royal entourage stop at Capilano Road to receive gifts and to present their own queen, Mary Agnes Capilano. She stood on the roadside, in full ceremonial regalia, with her son Chief Joe Mathias, who had attended the coronation of King George VI in 1911 and who would cast the first Aboriginal ballot in B.C. in 1949.

The royals didn't stop. Nobody from the Squamish Band was invited to take part in the honouring ceremony. "This was the only time that we could present my grandmother to the Queen," recalled Chief Simon Baker, "but the car drove past us. . . . It was terrible for my grandmother."

In a letter, the Honorary Secretary of the Vancouver Committee for the Reception of Their Majesties reassured the Squamish that their gifts were sent to Buckingham Palace. "We can assure you that every effort was made to fulfill the wishes of Their Majesties and had they desired to stop, it would have, of course, been done. We are assured that Their Majesties took particular pains to acknowledge the homage of their Indian subjects, and that in passing them the rate of speed was considerably lowered."

GEORGE HUNT

First employed as an interpreter for Commissioner Israel Powell in 1879, George Hunt greatly assisted photographer Edward S. Curtis with the filming of *In the Land of the Head-Hunters*, serving as Curtis' staging director, costume supplier and casting director from 1911 to 1914.

More importantly, George Hunt worked for 45 years as an informant and translator for the anthropologist Franz Boas, supplying artifacts and stories from 1888 until Hunt's death at Fort Rupert in September of 1933. Although Hunt is seldom credited as an author, the vast majority of Franz Boas' work based on Kwak'wala-language research, such as *Kwakiutl Texts* (1905, 1906), was derived directly from Hunt's written reports.

In 1910 Boas asserted his authority with a preface that stated, "The following series of Kwakiutl tales was collected by me on various journeys to British Columbia. In Volumes III and X of the publications of the Jesup North Pacific Expedition I have published a considerable number of myths written down by Mr. George Hunt of Fort Rupert, B.C., who speaks Kwakiutl as his native language.

"These tales were written under my direction, and the language was revised by me phonetically, the text being dictated to me in part by Mr. Hunt, in part by other natives. Since all the texts contained in the Publications of the Jesup Expedition have been written down by the same individual, they present a certain uniformity of diction. In order to overcome this, I collected during the work of the Jesup Expedition, as well as at other times, tales from the lips of natives, and these present the necessary control material for checking the reliability of the language and form of the tales recorded by Mr. Hunt."

George Hunt (moustache) and family with German anthropologist Franz Boas (right)

George Hunt's father was a Hudson's Bay Company factor in Fort Rupert and his Tlingit mother was Mary Ebbetts Hunt, daughter of Chief Tongass in southern Alaska. Born in Fort Rupert on February 14, 1854, Hunt was raised among the Kwakiutl, not the Tlingit.

Hunt's most significant role as a go-between was a dubious one: it was George Hunt who purchased the Yuquot Whalers' Shrine or Washing House from two chiefs at Friendly Cove, Nootka Sound, for $500 in 1904. He had first seen the Whalers' Shrine in 1903. Following instructions from Boas in New York, Hunt dismantled the centuries-old Yuquot "temple" located on a tiny island in Jewitt Lake, behind Yuquot and hastily packed 88 carved human figures for delivery to the American Museum of Natural History where Boas was a curator. Along with these carvings and the skulls of great whalers, Hunt sent 68 pages of narratives pertaining to the site.

Hunt had gained access to the sacred site by assuring the Mowachaht he was a shaman. After a sick Aboriginal was brought to Hunt and the man recovered, Hunt was granted permission to visit and photograph the wooden figures that puzzled early explorers such as James Cook in 1778 and Camille de Roquefeuil in 1817. More than any literate person before and probably since, George Hunt was able to glean some understanding of the shrine's spiritual power and the cultural significance of its ghostly figures.

Hunt described the Yuquot Whalers' Shrine as "the best thing that I ever bought from the Indians." Unfortunately for Hunt and history, Boas left the American Museum of Natural History in 1905 in the wake of some friction with its administrators. The intricate shrine was never re-assembled for public viewing. (In 1992, a documentary film crew brought Mowachaht band members to New York City to view the Whalers' Shrine in the museum's storeroom. This visit has given rise to a formal request by the Nuu-chah-nulth to have the relics returned to Yuquot, the ancestral summer home of Chief Maquinna.)

By 1910, Hunt's main employer, Franz Boas, had become suspicious that Hunt was using his acquisition budget "for purposes other than collecting"—such as potlatching. Even though he himself was a special constable, Hunt was once charged with, but acquitted of, violating a clause of the anti-potlatch law that prohibited the "mutilation of human bodies." Twice married to Kwakiutl wives, Hunt was intimate with the secret Hamatsa society rituals. Hunt was occasionally criticized by Boas as "unbelievably clumsy" and "hard to deal with" and "too lazy to use his brain" but such comments probably reveal more about Boas than his assistant.

Other Aboriginal or Métis ethnographers in the burgeoning field of anthropology undoubtedly experienced similar condescension from their patrons. Some of Hunt's peers in this regard were James Beynon (Tsimshian), Francis La Flesche (Omaha),

Arthur C. Parker (Seneca), J.N.B. Hewitt (Iroquois), Jesse Cornplanter (Seneca), Essie Parrish (Pomo), John Joseph Mathews (Osage), William Jones (Fox), James R. Murie (Pawnee) and Ella Deloria (a Yankton Sioux who was a student of Boas at Columbia University). Full-blooded Aboriginals who collected artifacts for study in B.C. included Henry Moody, Charles Edenshaw, Charles Nowell and Louis Shotridge.

MOURNING DOVE

"We are between two fires, the Red and the White. . . .
We are maligned and traduced as no one but we of the despised breeds
can know." —MOURNING DOVE, IN *COGEWEA, THE HALF-BLOOD*

Until the rediscovery of S. Alice Callahan's *Wynema: A Child of the Forest*, published in 1891, Mourning Dove's *Cogewea, The Half-Blood* (1927) was long considered the first novel written by an American Aboriginal woman.

Mourning Dove was born in a canoe on the Kootenai River, near Bonner's Ferry, Idaho, in 1888. Having lived and taught briefly near Oliver in the Okanagan Valley, the American-born writer is particularly significant in B.C. because she inspired her great-great-niece, Jeannette Armstrong of Penticton, sometimes regarded as Canada's first Aboriginal female novelist.

"There are two things I am most grateful for in my life," Mourning Dove once wrote. "The first is that I was born a descendant of the genuine Americans, the Indians; the second, that my birth happened in the year 1888.

"In that year the Indians of my tribe, the Colvile (Swy-ayl-puh), were well into the cycle of history involving their readjustment in living conditions. They were in a pathetic state of turmoil caused by trying to learn how to till the soil for a living, which was being done on a very small and crude scale. It was no easy matter for members of this aboriginal stock, accustomed to making a different livelihood (by the bow and arrow), to handle the plow and sow seed for food. Yet I was born long enough ago to have known people who lived in the ancient way before everything started to change."

The meaning of her Aboriginal name Hum-ishu-ma was lost to Mourning Dove. She later concluded its English translation as "Morning Dove" was a contrivance. Women within the Okanogon [sic] tribes of Washington State and the Okanagans in southern British Columbia were not traditionally named after birds or animals.

"The whiteman must have invented the name for it," she wrote in a letter in 1926. Morning Dove altered the spelling of her pen name to Mourning Dove after visiting a Spokane bird exhibit around 1921 and seeing a mounted bird that was labeled mourning dove. "I have made a sad mistake," she wrote. "I have misspelt my name. I found out at the museum."

According to her memoirs, Mourning Dove initially knew herself as Christal Quintasket but this name was incorrectly recorded by the Bureau of Indian Affairs as Christine Quintasket. Mourning Dove used the surname Quintasket because her father Joseph, orphaned at age nine, had apparently accepted the name of an Aboriginal stepfather. Initially the Quintaskets followed seasonal migration patterns, bringing horses north to Osoyoos Lake each year.

Born south of Kelowna on the east side of Okanagan Lake, Joseph Quintasket was a member of the Okanagan tribe; his mother Pat-tah-heets-sa was a Nicola medicine woman living among the Okanagan. Her mother Lucy Stukin was a member of the Colville (Salishan) tribe and her maternal grandfather was Chief Seewhelken.

Mourning Dove sometimes said that her paternal grandfather was a Scot, named Andrew, who had worked for the Hudson's Bay Company, but it has been suggested she might have claimed a white relative in order to improve her appeal as an author reli-

Mourning Dove's autobiography was published more than 50 years after her death.

ant upon a mainly white readership.

Two members of Mourning Dove's extended family were important to her in her formative years. From Jimmy Ryan, a thirteen-year-old white runaway orphan brought home and raised as a son by her father, she learned the alphabet and the pleasures of reading penny-dreadful novels.

"I could spell the word Kentucky before I ever had a primer because it occurred frequently in the novel Jimmy taught me from," she recalled. From Long Theresa or Teequalt, an elderly woman found wandering in the bush and waiting to die, Mourning Dove received her pubertal training and spiritual guidance (after Teequalt had been persuaded to join their family).

Teequalt would later serve Mourning Dove as the model for the second-most important character in her novel. Mourning Dove recalled, "She was twelve when she first heard of the new people [whites] coming into our country in boats instead of canoes. When my parents went for game or berries, we children took care of her. We prepared meals according to her instructions, then we would sit at her feet and listen to her wonderful stories."

At age seven, as Christal Quintasket, Mourning Dove was placed in the Sacred Heart School at the Goodwin Mission in Ward, near Kettle Falls, Washington. There she was cruelly treated by nuns who punished her for speaking Salishan. After being sent home, she returned and took her first communion in 1899. "My second stay at the school was less traumatic," she recalled. "I was anxious to learn more English and read."

When government funding for Aboriginal schools was rescinded, she and her classmates were moved to a school at Fort Spokane. In 1902, at age fourteen, she was sent home again, this time to look after her four younger sisters and two younger brothers after her mother died, supposedly as the result of sorcery involving the skewered body of a dried black toad. Two of her sisters died.

"I began secretly to read Jimmy's books," she recalled. "My parents scolded and rebuked me many times because they thought reading was an excuse for being idle."

Upon her father's remarriage, Mourning Dove was sent to another school for Aboriginals in Great Falls, Montana, where she witnessed the last roundup of the buffalo herd in 1908. There she married Hector McLeod, a Flathead who proved himself to be an abusive husband. Having had his arm shot off by a bootlegger, Hector McLeod was later shot to death during a card game in Shurz, Nevada, in 1937.

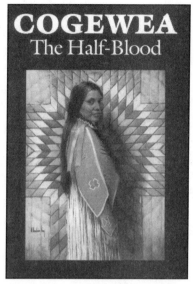

In her late teens, Mourning Dove went to live with her maternal grandmother from whom she learned the power of Okanagan storytelling. Mourning Dove's exposure to western pulp novels also influenced her approach to writing fiction. In particular, she was motivated by a 1909 novel by Theresa Broderick entitled *The Brand: A Tale of the Flathead Reservation.*

By 1912 Mourning Dove was living in Portland and writing her novel, frustrated by her difficulties with English. Eager for advancement, she enrolled herself in typing and writing courses at a business college in Calgary, Alberta between 1913 and 1915. Thereafter she taught school at the Inkameep Indian Reserve at Oliver, B.C., where she saved enough of her salary to buy herself a typewriter.

Mourning Dove's literary aspirations were heightened when she met her mentor, editor and co-writer Lucullus Virgil McWhorter at Walla Walla Frontier Days in Washington State, probably in 1915. An ethnologist who was adopted into the Yakima tribe after his vigorous defence of their irrigation rights, McWhorter was a sincere student of Aboriginal cultures who had received the honorary name He-mene Ka-wan, meaning "Old Wolf."

Also the founder of *American Archaeologist*, McWhorter had moved to a Washington State homestead from his native West Virginia in 1903. A mutual friend named J.W. Langdon advised Mourning Dove to pursue McWhorter's collaboration. While she re-worked her novel and he added his own didactic passages, McWhorter encouraged her to gather more Okanagan stories.

Mourning Dove became an advisor to local chiefs until she married Fred Galler, a Wenatchee, in 1919. Although this marriage was happier than her first, her subsequent domestic life as an itinerant fruit and vegetable picker proved extremely difficult. Childless, she lugged her typewriter with her, camping out in hop fields and apple orchards, exhausted much of the time.

Mourning Dove had to wait 15 years after meeting McWhorter before her long-in-progress novel *Cogewea, The Half Blood: A Depiction of the Great Montana Cattle Range* was finally published. The title was misleading. Although the novel includes recollections of the final buffalo roundup, it mainly concerns three sisters: Mary is traditional, Julia has assimilated into white culture and the halfblood Cogewea seeks a compromise between two cultures.

At first Cogewea declines the opportunity to marry the villainous Densmore. She knows white men notoriously deflower, devalue and deceive their non-white partners. Contrary to her grandmother's advice, she eventually elopes with Densmore and deals with the consequences of estrangement by seeking solace within the customs of her "Indian Spirit" with the help of the "semi-civilized" oral historian of the Okanogans named Stem-tee-ma, meaning grandmother. More than 100 years old, Stem-tee-ma passes along tribal traditions and emphasizes the importance of storytelling.

Despite some recognition that arose with the release of *Cogewea*, Mourning Dove's life remained harsh. Her status as an Aboriginal novelist and her ownership of a Ford jalopy did not prevent her from suffering pneumonia, rheumatism and other illnesses that arose from exhaustion. Increasingly active in Aboriginal politics, she gave public talks, started social organizations such as the Colville Indian Association, and secured monies owed to the tribe, but the only formal recognition she received for her writing was an honorary membership in the Eastern Washington State Historical Society.

Again with McWhorter's assistance, Mourning Dove's *Coyote Stories* (1933) appeared with credit for editing and illustrations accorded to Heister Dean Guie. Neither McWhorter nor Guie fully trusted Mourning Dove as an authority on Okanagan culture but she was allowed to provide an introduction that placed her work in an Okanagan context. A foreword by Chief Standing Bear was added by her editors because he was having contemporaneous success with his own books about the Sioux. *Coyote Stories* contains stories such as "The Spirit Chief Names the Animal People" about the coyote tradition and the concept of power emanating from the Sweat House ritual, but most of Mourning Dove's writing was mangled and overly sanitized by her editor.

McWhorter would indirectly play a role in the publication of Mourning Dove's only other book, *Mourning Dove: A Salishan Autobiography*, (1990), edited by Jay Miller, after her manuscript for the memoir was discovered by McWhorter's widow almost a half-century after her death.

In July of 1936, Mourning Dove was taken to the state hospital at Medical Lake in Washington State where she died at age forty-eight. The death certificate stated the cause of death was exhaustion from manic depression. Until recently, her gravestone said only "Mrs. Fred Galler."

Coyote Stories

By Mourning Dove *(Hu-mis'-hu-ma)*

Edited and illustrated by Heister Dean Guie with notes by L. V. McWhorter *(Old Wolf)* and a foreword by Chief Standing Bear, Oglala Sioux

The CAXTON PRINTERS, Ltd.
CALDWELL, IDAHO
1934

WILLIAM HENRY PIERCE

"Before the Gospel was preached by the Missionary, the natives were ignorant, superstititous, degraded, wild and cruel."—WILLIAM PIERCE

Born on June 10, 1856, at Fort Rupert on Vancouver Island, William Henry Pierce was the son of a Scottish fur trader and a Tsimshian woman who died three weeks after his birth. He was taken from his father by his maternal grandfather and "brought up amongst the Indians" until he went to sea as a cabin boy on the Hudson's Bay steamer *Otter* at age twelve.

Influenced as a child by the Metlahkatla mission of William Duncan, Pierce committed himself to Christ after hearing Thomas Crosby speak in Victoria. Pierce was ordained in 1887 and became a Methodist missionary on the Nass River and at Bella Bella. Stationed at Port Essington in 1910, Pierce helped organize the Native Fishing Society prior to his retirement to Prince Rupert in 1933.

Edited by Reverend J.P. Hicks and printed in Vancouver, the memoir or "auto-sketch," *From Potlatch to Pulpit, Being the Autobiography of Rev. William Henry Pierce* (1933), was written at the request of missionary authorities in Toronto. This rare written account of a Métis missionary concludes with Pierce's return to work at Port Essington in 1910. The final one-third outlines Aboriginal cultural practices prior to European influences.

William H. Pierce

William Pierce died in 1948. The Pierce Memorial Church at Kispiox, B.C., is named for him.

CHARLES NOWELL

Written prior to an era when academics were self-censored by political correctness, *Smoke from Their Fires: The Life of a Kwakiutl Chief* (1941) is a refreshingly frank and classic autobiography of Kwakiutl Chief Charles James Nowell, co-produced with Clellan S. Ford of Yale University, when Nowell was age seventy. (Ford received preliminary guidance for the project from Franz Boas but he remains better known around the world for co-writing *Patterns of Sexual Behavior* in 1951.)

Based on interviews conducted in 1940, *Smoke from Their Fires* includes a 40-page introduction to Kwakiutl culture and some candid comments from Nowell about sexual behaviour and family customs such as child care. Drawings were contributed by Alfred Shaughnessy from Kingcome.

Born in 1870 at Fort Rupert, Nowell acquired the name Charles James from Reverend Hall while attending the Anglican school at Alert Bay. He married the daughter of Nimpkish chief Lagius around 1895 and received the name Hamdzidagame ("you are the man that feeds other people"). In 1899 he began assisting freelance museum collector Charles Frederick Newcombe by offering to collect skeletons for him. Despite some antagonism between the two men, Newcombe persuaded Nowell to be among a group of Kwakiutl and Nootka who attended an exhibition held in St. Louis in 1904. Their entourage included Nowell's friend Bob Harris from Fort Rupert, the shaman Ateu (or Atlieu), his daughter Annie Ateu and others.

In Chicago, Chief Charley demonstrated the harness that restrains a Hamatsa dancer.

Nowell and his companions appeared in ceremonial regalia at the fairgrounds at Forest Park, five miles west of the Mississippi River, as representatives of the "singularly light-colored fisherfolk" of Vancouver Island. Afterwards Newcombe brought Nowell, Ateu and Harris to Chicago for a month where they proved themselves useful by identifying and describing Kwakiutl materials that had been gathered by the museum.

Ford's rendering of Nowell's fascinating life story, *Smoke from Their Fires*, is a landmark volume in B.C. non-fiction, the first full-length biography presented in the form of an autobiography.

WILLIAM SEPASS

*"In 1943 he passed into the Great Beyond, leaving behind a
record of achievement unsurpassed by any Indian of his time."*
—OLIVER N. WELLS

Reputedly born in the 1840s at Kettle Falls, Washington, around the time touring artist Paul Kane recorded the presence of a Chief Sepayss, Chief of the Waters, the remarkable Chilliwack Chief William Sepass (aka K'HHalserten, meaning Golden Snake) of Skowkale, near Sardis in the Fraser Valley, is rarely cited in any literary context, but it is possible Sepass is the earliest-born Aboriginal author of British Columbia.

As a boy, Sepass accompanied his tribe north into the Fraser Canyon, in the wake of an epidemic in Washington, and he was soon selected and trained to become the custodian of family and tribal knowledge. During the Cariboo gold rush, Sepass' father built a freight canoe out of a cedar log to transport miners and their prospecting supplies across Chilliwack Lake. Sepass' mother was the daughter of a Thompson River chief.

Around the time British Columbia became a colony, Sepass' people, the Tcilqeuk or Tsilli-way-ukhs, became known as the Chilliwacks, a name that Sepass later maintained was derived from the word Tsilli-way-ukh, meaning Gathering Place of the People of K'HHalls, the Sun God. Fanciful attempts have been made to link Sepass, or Y-Ail-Mihth, meaning The Ancient Singer, with sun-worshipping peoples who ostensibly migrated northward from Central America and Mexico.

Sepass' first wife Rose, the daughter of Thompson Uslick, bore him eight children but most of them died of tuberculosis. Particularly distraught about the death of his son Eddie, Sepass

Chief William Sepass with his first wife Rose

carved a headpiece on his son's grave, as encouraged by Reverend Thomas Crosby. The inscription read simply, "Eddie. 1880–1886."

Widely respected as a powerful orator, Sepass was also touted as an unsurpassed canoe-maker and a renowned hunter. Because he became partially literate, William ("Indian Billy") Sepass was encouraged by the Indian Affairs Department to serve as spokesman for his people. He forcefully represented the land claims of the Stó:lo people to the 1913 Royal Commission and he was an active dairy farmer in the Native Farmers Association.

Concerned that his people were losing touch with their heritage, Sepass decided he wanted his stories to be preserved "in the Whiteman's book." He consequently related 15 traditional songs for posterity between 1911 and 1915. During four years of patient translation, Sepass recorded his songs in a rhythmic form, including a Stó:lo version of the genesis of the world.

The narrative songs were translated for him, from the Salish, by Sophia Jane White, daughter of Reverend Edward White, a Wesleyan missionary who had arrived in the Lower Fraser Valley in 1867. Having grown up in the Fraser Valley, Sophia White was educated in Ontario but she had returned to the Chilliwack area and married a settler named Charles Sibbald Lockwood Street.

Mrs. C.L. Street entrusted the publication of the manuscript to her daughter, Eloise Street Harries, who edited *Indian Time* magazine. Excerpts first appeared in the *Native Voice* newspaper in the late 1940s. For her rudimentary mimeographed versions, such as *Sepass Poems* (1955) and *The Songs of Y-Ail-Mihth* (1958), Eloise Street incorporated a charcoal sketch of Sepass done by Vancouver artist Ada Currie Robertson around 1931.

In additional versions Street added photographs of key participants, a somewhat preposterous preface by Chief Shup-She, aka Howard Lyle La Hurreau, of Fort Wayne, Indiana, and a lengthy introduction by amateur ethnographer Oliver Wells, a third-generation farmer whose family had long been intimate friends with Sepass. Writing the introduction to Sepass' posthumous book was a turning point in the life of Oliver Wells, prompting him to begin his alternate career as an ethnographer.

The important relationship between the Wells family at their Edenbank farm and Chief Sepass was predated by the relationship of Chief Sepass with the White/Street family. It was Reverend White who first recommended to the Methodist Church that a permanent missionary should be sent to the Chilliwack River, whereupon the young Reverend Thomas Crosby was duly sent from Nanaimo in a dugout canoe in January of 1869.

Able to speak the Halkomelem language fluently, Crosby, later a famous missionary on the West Coast, recorded meeting Sepass in his memoirs, published in 1907, and supposedly converted William Sepass to Christianity.

Charcoal drawing of Chief Sepass by Ada Currie Robertson, 1931

Around 1934 or 1935, William Sepass told anthropologist Diamond Jenness the story of why the Chilliwacks would not eat oolachan.

"Once the only salmon that came up the Fraser River was the steelhead. Beaver and some companions made a weir in the Chilliwack River to catch them. When the others had set their bag nets there was no room for Beaver's, so he dug a trench at one end. They caught many salmon and ate them on the spot, taking none home to their wives.

"The women sent a boy down to the weir to see what their husbands were doing. He pretended to be chasing butterflies, but unseen, he tied two bunches of salmon eggs round his legs like short leggings and went home. When the women asked him what the men were doing he said, 'They have caught a lot of salmon and are eating them. See, I have brought you some of the eggs that were hung up to dry.' Then the women were very angry. They pounded up cedar-bark and made from it belts, and head-bands for themselves. Then they lashed together two canoes, dressed themselves up, put quantities of down on their heads, and with two women paddling, went off to find their husbands.

"The wind blew the down from their heads towards the men, who sent out two of their number—two Woodpeckers of different species—to fly up the river and see who was coming. When they reported back, the men debated what they should do. Their leader said, 'We had better go away to the home of the Salmon and steal their babies.' They embarked in a canoe, Beaver, Mouse, the two Woodpeckers, and two *yuwilmat* [Aboriginal doctors] who know how to make fine weather, and they paddled far away to where the sky alternately dips down to earth and rises again, causing the tides. The yuwilmat prayed to the sky to move slowly so that they would have time to pass under it without being caught. They passed under, and approached some houses, the home of the Salmon. As they drew near Beaver jumped overboard, after arranging with the two Woodpeckers to fly after him when he had drawn the attention of the Salmon. He swam to shore, and lay at the edge of the waves, seemingly dead.

"The Salmon people came out of their houses and called to one another, 'Have you ever seen a creature like this before?' None of them recognized him. At last they said, 'Let us call Coho.' Coho walked down to the beach and examined Beaver. 'Oh yes,' he said, 'I know him. It is Beaver. He dug a trench up on the Chilliwack River in which to set his net. Bring me a knife and I will cut him open to see what is inside him.' Someone went for a knife, while Beaver lay praying that the Woodpeckers would arrive in time. Just as Coho received the knife the woodpeckers landed on the beach behind the people, who turned to look at them. 'What beautiful creatures,' they exclaimed. 'Let us catch them.' They all tried to catch them, but the Woodpeckers eluded them. While their attention was thus distracted, Beaver and Mouse entered their houses, and while Beaver searched for their richest baby, Mouse ate their bow-strings, the lashing of their weapons, and bored holes in their canoes. Beaver found the baby of Sockeye, the prince of the Salmon, and, tucking it under his arm, fled to the canoe.

"Mouse and the Woodpeckers joined him and they fled away to the Fraser River, the Salmon being unable to overtake them because their canoes leaked too badly. They put the head-pad of the baby in the Chilliwack River; that is why sockeye are so plentiful there, and so good to eat. Farther up towards Yale they placed its diaper; sockeye are plentiful there also, but are not so good to eat. The baby itself they set at the bottom of a deep hole in the River near Yale. You can still see it there at low water— a rock that exactly resembles a human being and seems to have long hair on its head.

"Meanwhile the Salmon discussed what they should do. Sockeye said, 'We had better follow them.' Humpback announced that he would follow them on the morrow, which meant the next year. So Sockeye and the other salmon went up the Fraser River, and the Humpback followed them a year later.

"The women then debated what they would do. They decided to go down to the salt water, but before leaving they threw an old couple, a man and a woman, into two creeks that unite at Vedder Crossing. You can see them there today—two rocks, one in one creek, one in the other. Children used to be warned to keep away from them, for if flies gathered round these rocks they would become sick. When the women reached the salt water they leaped and changed into oolachan. That is why the Chilliwack Indians would not eat oolachan."

GORDON ROBINSON

In Haisla, "Kitamaat" means People of the Snow; it also refers to the village located across the bay from the newer city of Kitimat. Born in the village of Kitamaat on October 1, 1918, Gordon Robinson published a collection of traditional Haisla stories, *Tales of Kitamaat* (1956). Prior to their collective publication, illustrated by Vincent Haddelsey and introduced by Stanley Rough, Robinson's articles and stories about his people had appeared in the *Kitimat Northern Sentinel.*

"He wrote down stories he didn't want people to forget," his niece Eden Robinson told *Quill & Quire* in 2000, "but he got some flack for it. He was told, 'You're not supposed to write them down.' All our stories are oral. Other than that book, you're not going to find any books about the Haisla."

Some of the local monsters that are referenced in Eden Robinson's first novel were named by her uncle in 1956 as Sahnis the water grizzly and the Jesee Lake monster, as well as a gigantic octopus, "as large as a steamboat," called the Monster of

Gordon Robinson

Sue Passage. In addition to legends and folklore, Gordon Robinson explains the importance of oolachan oil for trading and potlatch purposes, he describes a meeting between Captain George Vancouver and Katsilanoo the clown, and he recalls the importance of lay Aboriginal minister Charles Amos who converted to Christianity in 1876. As well, he translates numerous Haisla sayings such as, "Mimic a lame, blind, palsied or otherwise unfortunate person and you will in time acquire the affliction yourself."

Gordon Robinson attended the Coqualeetza Residential School in Sardis and gained his teaching diploma from the Provincial Normal School in Vancouver. He taught in Kitamaat for five years and served as chief councillor at his village from 1950 to 1954. In 1949 he became Assistant Superintendent of the Kwakiutl Indian Agency at Alert Bay but he returned to Kitamaat in 1950 to work for the Aluminum Company of Canada (Alcan) in its personnel department.

WALTER WRIGHT

"And with the coming of the men whose skins are white like the peeled willow stick there have come many new modes of life."—WALTER WRIGHT

Medeek is the Tsimshian word for grizzly bear. The grizzly bear is a crest that belongs to the Gitselasu Killer Whale clan family that includes the lineage of Walter Wright, who learned the history of Medeek from his grandfather, Neas Hiwas. "In the Native tongue," Walter Wright wrote, "it takes eight hours to tell. So, several times each year, I sat at his feet and listened to our records. I drank in the words. In time I became word perfect. I knew all the story. I could repeat it without missing any of its parts."

In 1935 and 1936, Chief Walter Wright, at age sixty-five, narrated the tribal history and laws of the Kitselas band in the land of Ksan to Will Robinson, a local amateur ethnologist, for transcription into two proposed books, *Men of Medeek* (1962) and *The Wars of Medeek* (unpublished).

As a non-Aboriginal, Will Robinson had come to Terrace in 1928. He once described his informant Walter Wright as "a man of marked intelligence—and shrewdness. He was willing to give information—up to a certain point. I sensed he wished to know me better before he spoke more freely."

The partnership between Wright and Robinson commenced in September of 1935 when Wright came to Robinson's home and told him the story of the Goat Feast for two-and-a-half hours.

Wright died in 1941 and Will Robinson died in 1953, having been unable to find a publisher. Robinson's wife continued to search for a publication outlet until Stan Rough heard about the manuscript from some friends in Terrace in 1960 and asked Mrs. Barry Blix and Gordon Robinson, the author of *Tales of Kitamaat*, to confirm its merit.

Stan Rough sought a publisher but again the project was perceived to have limited sales potential. Ultimately Rough approached the editor of the *Kitimat Northern Sentinel* newspaper, Pixie Meldrum, who arranged for *Men of Medeek* to be printed in Kitimat. Financed by a number of private donors, it contains a good deal of description of inter-tribal warfare.

Walter Wright

In October of 2003, Barry Robinson, the grandson of the non-Aboriginal co-author Will Robinson, presented the Kitselas First Nation with the original manuscripts versions of *The Men of Medeek* and the unpublished work, *The Wars of Medeek*.

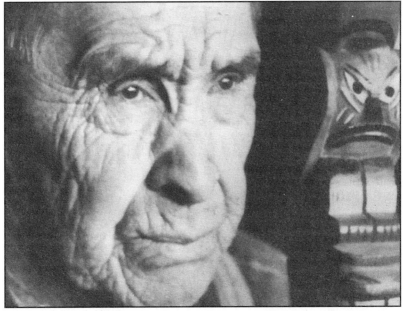

Domanic Charlie, at age eighty-five, enrolled in Grade One to learn to read and write.

DOMANIC CHARLIE

Oliver Wells' interviews with half-brothers Domanic Charlie and August Jack Khahtsahlano formed the basis for *Squamish Legends . . . The First People* (1966), a slim collection published by Charles Chamberlain, proprietor of the Tomahawk Cafe in North Vancouver where August Jack Khahtsahlano's carvings were offered for sale.

Primarily concerned with the origins of the Squamish people, this illustrated volume concludes with both men's versions of how the legendary sea serpent of Burrard Inlet (*SAY-nohs-KIY) was killed. Wells' first ethnographic excursion beyond Chilliwack had occurred on July 9, 1965, when he travelled to the Yekwaupsum Indian Reserve (No. 18), north of Squamish, to the ancestral home of August Jack Khahtsahlano's mother.

As the son of Jericho Charlie (shin-AHL-tset), hereditary Squamish Chief Domanic Charlie was reputedly born in 1866 and baptized near Jericho Beach in Vancouver on December 25, 1885. He worked for August Jack Khahtsahlano booming logs down the Serpentine River, as a boom man at the mouth of the Squamish River, then for nine years in a North Vancouver mill.

"He [Domanic Charlie] is a member of the *SKWIY-kway dance Society," Oliver Wells wrote, "and continues to practice 'good medicine' as one of the few remaining Indian Doctors with a full knowledge of herbal plant medicine and its use." In old age, Domanic Charlie was renowned as a weather forecaster.

Although his first name was generally spelled Dominic, it was recorded as Domanic Charlie on the book jacket of his only publication. He died in North Vancouver on September 9, 1972.

AUGUST JACK KHAHTSAHLANO

Squamish Chief August Jack Khahtsahlano was born near the site of Burrard Bridge in Vancouver at the village of Snauq (or Snaug) on July 16, 1867, and baptized in 1879. Spellings of his surname are varied. The suffix lan-o or lan-ogh means "man." He distributed 100 blankets at a memorable potlatch in 1900 after inheriting his name from his grandfather Chief Khahtsahlano of Sun'ahk. A former sawmill worker, he formally became August Jack Khahtsahlano in 1938. From 1932 onwards, archivist Major J.S. Matthews recorded some of his stories and personal history for *Conversations with Khatsalano 1932–1954* (1969), a follow-up to *Squamish Legends* with Oliver Wells.

The name of Kitsilano as a neighbourhood was appropriated by the Canadian Pacific Railway after consultations with local post-

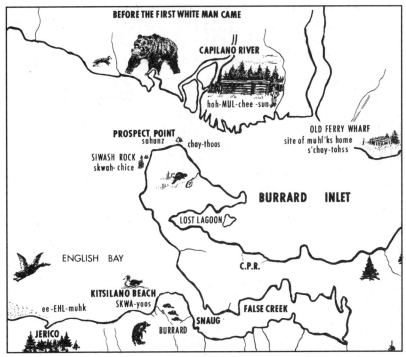

BEFORE THE FIRST WHITE MAN CAME

CAPILANO RIVER

hoh-MUL-chee-sun

PROSPECT POINT
sahunz   chay-thoos

SIWASH ROCK
skwah-chice

OLD FERRY WHARF
site of muhl'ks home
s'chay-tohss

BURRARD   INLET

LOST LAGOON

ENGLISH   BAY

C.P.R.

KITSILANO BEACH
ee-EHL-muhk   SKWA-yoos

FALSE CREEK

SNAUG

JERICO   BURRARD

Map of "Indian villages and landmarks" from Squamish Legends

master Jonathan Miller who, in turn, consulted ethnographer
Charles Hill-Tout. By the 1890s, the village of Snauq was sur-
rounded by land owned by Donald Smith and Richard Angus of
the CPR, and land developers David Oppenheimer, C.D. Rand
and R.G. Tatlow. The B.C. government pushed through an arrangement to buy 72 acres (Kitsilano Reserve No. 6), without
federal authority, in March of 1913, for $218,750, whereupon
Khahtsahlano and his people were moved to North Vancouver's
Capilano Reserve. The federal government protested the deal
for the Snauq area (now known as Vanier Park). Conservative
MP H.H. Stevens convinced Ottawa to buy out the province's
acquisition.

Chief August Jack Khahtsahlano died in Vancouver on June
14, 1967. After the Squamish people launched a retroactive legal
appeal in 1976, the federal government proposed a $92.5 mil-
lion trust as compensation in 2000, but it was not accepted.

The eccentric Vancouver archivist Major J.S. Matthews once sent the following memo about August Jack Khahtsahlano to ethnologist Oliver Wells.

Son of Khaytulk, or "Supple Jack" of Chaythoos, and grandson of Chief Khahtsahlanogh (no European name) in whose honour the suburb Kitsilano, Vancouver, is named. On 12th February, 1879, he was baptized by Rev. Fathyer N. Gregane, as "Auguste fils de Shinaotset and de Menatloot, Squamishs, baptise l'age d'environ 12 mois le 12, Février, 1879." August stated 16th July, 1946: "Auguste!! that's me. When I little boy they call me 'Menatlot' (pronounced men-at-el-ot). But priest make mistake. My father Khay-tulk, he die day I was born. Qwy-what, my mother, marry Chinoatset (usually spelled Chinalset, i.e., 'Jericho Charlie', a very good man), whose first wife was Menatelot." The original baptismal certificate is in City Archives, deposited by August. August was born at the vanished Indian village of Shaug (False Creek Indian Reserve) in a lodge directly below the present Burrard Bridge. At this Squamish village, in a big long lodge of Toe-wyo-quam-kee and by Squamish rite, in the presence of a large assemblage of his tribe and visiting Indians from Musqueam, Nanaimo, Sechelt and Ustlawn (North Vancouver), the patronymic of his grandfather 'Khaht-sah-lah-nogh' was conferred upon him

Chief August Jack Khahtsahlano

with ceremony by a Squamish patriarch, and that of Kaytulk, their father, upon his brother, Willie. They were both young men, and August, having acquired wealth by working in a nearby sawmill, returned the compliment by giving a potlatch, at which he distributed to the assembled guests, men, women, and children, over one hundred blankets, and other valuables, and also provided a feast. It took place about 1900. . . . August is a wise man, a courteous gentleman, and a natural historian.

George Clutesi and his publisher Gray Campbell

GEORGE CLUTESI

Born in Port Alberni in 1905, George Clutesi was a shy child whose mother died when he was age four. A member of the Tse-Shaht band, he endured residential school; worked as a pile driver, labourer and fisherman for 20 years; and took up painting and writing after he broke his back working in construction.

While receiving treatments in Vancouver, Clutesi met Ira Dilworth, Vancouver's chief executive at CBC, who was one of Emily Carr's few close friends. Dilworth encouraged Clutesi to refine his writing for a series of CBC radio broadcasts. Although they had not known one another long before she died in Victoria in 1945, Emily Carr bequeathed her brushes, oils and blank canvasses to George Clutesi in her will.

By 1947, Clutesi, as a father of five, was broadcasting traditional Aborginal stories for young listeners on CBC, province-wide. He followed Chief Dan George as an actor in films and he became the first B.C.-born Aboriginal to gain broad acceptance as an author of Aboriginal stories.

In 1947, Clutesi also began contributing inspirational essays on Aboriginal culture to the *Native Voice*, a newly formed Aboriginal newspaper. The *Native Voice* published transcriptions of Clutesi's "folk lore of the Seshaht tribe which have been handed down from father to son for generations."

By 1949, Clutesi was sufficiently well-regarded and self-confident to hitchhike from Port Alberni to Victoria to address Rt. Hon. Vincent Massey, chairman of the Royal Commission on National Development of Arts, Letters & Sciences, during the Commission's two-day meetings at the Legislative Buildings.

POTLATCH

GEORGE CLUTESI

Illustrations by the Author

GRAY'S PUBLISHING LTD., SIDNEY, BRITISH COLUMBIA, CANADA

Sidney-based publisher Gray Campbell once recalled that when he heard about Clutesi, he went to the Port Alberni Indian Reserve and found Clutesi atop his house, fixing his roof. Understandably wary of white men after his experiences in the Port Alberni Residential School, George Clutesi wouldn't come down from his roof.

Undaunted, Gray Campbell climbed up the ladder. The men had a long talk but no arrangements were made as to how they might proceed. Almost a year later, Clutesi telephoned from the Vancouver Airport. He said he was thinking over what Campbell had said up on the roof.

Campbell conceived *Son of Raven, Son of Deer* (1967) as a Centennial Project with Morriss Printing of Victoria. With the assistance of a freelance editor, Clutesi's *Son of Raven, Son of Deer* (1967) became a cornerstone of Aboriginal literature of B.C. (Among the 61 titles Campbell released between 1962 and 1982, Campbell also published *Tales from the Longhouse* (1973), a collection of stories for children, gathered from Aboriginal elders, on behalf of the B.C. Indian Arts Society.) Including 18 original illustrations, Clutesi's collection of 12 fables became commercially successful partially because Campbell undertook a promotional tour with Clutesi, introducing him to media personalities.

In 1967, Clutesi created a large mural for the Indian Pavilion at Expo '67 in Montreal. In doing so, Clutesi, as a painter and author, became the first Aboriginal artist to gain widespread recognition in British Columbia after Pauline Johnson.

Clutesi followed his first collection of stories with *Potlatch* (1969), a work that dramatized the ritual of the potlatch. "You should have seen the old folks telling the stories when I was a boy," Clutesi once said. "They would act, dance and sing each part with changing voices." In his introduction to *Potlatch*, Clutesi claims the word potlatch was derived from the Nootka verb Pachitle, to give, in association with the noun Pa-chuk, in reference to an article to be given. It's one of various interpretations of the term. Again, an editor was hired by Gray Campbell to revise Clutesi's writing for publication.

In 1971, Clutesi was awarded an honorary degree by the University of Victoria. Thereafter he appeared as an actor in three movies: *Dreamspeaker* (1977), directed by Claude Jutra and written by Anne Cameron; *Nightwing* (1979), directed by Arthur Hiller; and *Prophecy* (1979), directed by John Frankenheimer. Clutesi received the Order of Canada and other awards and citations prior to his death in Victoria on February 27, 1988. A non-fiction book, *Stand Tall, My Son* (1990), appeared posthumously.

HOWARD ADAMS

Consistently outspoken, Howard Adams, a self-described halfbreed, gravitated to the West Coast where he became one of Canada's most provocative intellectuals.

A great-grandson of Maxime Lepine, a leading guerrilla warrior on the Riel Council during the Rebellion of 1885, Adams increasingly mistrusted and disdained a "collaborator class" of Métis, Inuit and Indian leaders. He recognized decades of "corruption, fraud and thieving by mafia Aboriginal organizations that pretend to represent Indian and Métis people." His uncensored rhetoric made him vulnerable to dismissal as a Red Power advocate as well as a threat to establishment figures within the Aboriginal community because he could think and write "outside of the box."

Author of *Prison of Grass: Canada from the Native Point of View* (1975) and the earlier *The Education of Canadians* (1968), Adams also wrote *A Tortured People: The Politics of Colonization* (1995) in which he looked with uncompromising anger at Canadian history through the prism of colonialism. He argued that Eurocentrism, as an instrument of camouflage and exploitation, was still very much alive. He believed the newly fashionable term First Nations was racist in tone, derivative of an imperial vocabulary that served to thwart the unification of Aboriginal communities.

Adams received his B.A. from UBC and his Ph.D. in Educational History in 1965 from Berkeley. As a professor at the University of Saskatchewan from 1965 to 1974, he was a self-described Red Power advocate who doubled as President of the Saskatchewan Métis Association from 1968 to 1970. Adams subsequently taught Native American Studies at the University of California from 1975 until his retirement in 1988, after which he lived primarily in Vancouver.

Born into a Métis family in St. Louis, Saskatchewan, in 1926, Adams recalled, "In school I was taught that we were retarded. I believed that I was dumb, in comparison to white students; and that I was low class, crude and dirty. . . . As a child in the ghetto, I knew my shame by looking 'Indian,' by living in a log shack, by eating bannock and lard. Hostility and violence emerged with self-hatred. The fact that I could not play on the village baseball team or hockey team because I was not white stung me deeply. . . . I was ragged, uncouth and I stunk. I did not belong to the level of the 'nice, proper, elegant' middle class. There were reasons, I told myself, why I should be treated differently. I lived in a low class colony. I did not speak the 'Standard English.'"

After completing his elementary and high school education in St. Louis, Adams served two-and-a-half years in the RCMP, worked for the Vancouver School Board as a probation officer, then gained his teaching credentials from the University of British Columbia. He taught school in Coquitlam, B.C., for six years.

As an Aboriginal historian who specialized in the development of more intellectual rigour in Aboriginal society, Adams was critical of the emphasis on traditional storytelling at the expense of rationalist dialogue and academic standards.

"I am deeply concerned," he said, "by the incredible lack of authentic Aboriginal historical writing."

Howard Adams died in Vancouver in 2001.

Howard Adams

JAMES SEWID

"I think the biggest problem to be solved and the most important is the land question. We are non-treaty Indians on the coast and I think we should be compensated for our land."—CHIEF JAMES SEWID

James Sewid was born in Alert Bay on December 31, 1913. The surname Sewid means "paddling towards the chief that is giving a potlatch." His paternal grandfather acquired the given name James because he had worked for Governor James Douglas. Soon after James Sewid's father was killed in a logging accident on Village Island in 1914, a large potlatch was held at Alert Bay during which James Sewid, as an infant, received several additional names including Owadzidi, meaning "people will do anything for him because he is so respected," and Poogleedee, meaning "guests never leave his feasts hungry." The latter phrase was repeated as the title of his autobiography *Guests Never Leave Hungry* (1969), prepared with the assistance of James P. Spradley, an assistant professor of psychiatry and anthropology at the University of Washington.

Raised on Village Island and at Alert Bay, James Sewid began to fish on his grandfather's boat at age twelve and married a high-ranking girl at age thirteen. He became a skipper in 1934 and bought his own fishing boat in 1940. In 1945 he moved his family from Village Island to Alert Bay where he became the first elected chief of the Nimpkish First Nation. Active in the Anglican Church, the Hamatsa Society and the politics of the Native Brotherhood of B.C., Sewid was selected in 1955 as the subject for a National Film Board documentary about reviving Aboriginal traditions called *No Longer Vanishing*.

Sewid was particularly influential in the revival of the potlatch

James Sewid

among the Kwakw<u>a</u>ka'wakw. " . . . and it just came to me," he
wrote, "that it would be a good idea to bring the potlatch custom
and the dancing out to the surface again and let the public see it
because it had been outlawed and lost. I had the idea that we
wouldn't go and do it the way they used to do it when they gave
people articles to come and watch the dancing. The way I fig-
ured it was going to be the other way around, like the theatres,
operas, or a good stage program which was put on and the people had to pay money to get in."

As one of the leading proponents of the Big House project at
Alert Bay, Sewid also organized representatives from other tribes
to create more interest in Indian crafts. "It will also give our young
people the chance to keep alive the culture of their people," he
said. Initial meetings were held with Simon Beans of Alert Bay,
Charles George of Blunden Harbour and Chief Henry Speck of
Turnour Island. Construction of the Big House began in 1964.

Chief James Sewid died at Campbell River on May 18, 1988.
His daughter Daisy Sewid-Smith of Campbell River has continued his legacy of constructive activism.

SKYROS BRUCE

Skyros Bruce's little-known *Kalala Poems* (1972) was published in a limited edition of 250 copies when she was twenty. Bruce's collection of 37 poems of alienation, loneliness and suicidal thoughts were introduced by her publisher Lionel Kearns, a Simon Fraser University English professor and poet who noted on the book jacket that her Aboriginal name in the Squamish band was Kalala, meaning butterfly. "She is talented and beautiful," he wrote, "but she has come this far through circumstances that can only be described as grim."

Raised in North Vancouver as a niece of Chief Dan George, Skyros Bruce was also known as Mary Bruce. Her brother was Andy Bruce, the central figure in a hostage-taking incident at the B.C. Penitentiary that resulted in a play called *Walls*, written by Christian Bruyère, and a 1984 movie of the same name, scripted by Bruyère and directed by Tom Shandel. She has written:

> *when they took you from me / with their beautiful blue serge suits we cried / they looked on / with willowy / all-wise / eyes / as you pulled the stockings / over your hands / with your closed eyes / we saw a gentle man, green / under the limber stalks / and i saw your life-force / moving / over / my womb / all they ever saw was a convict*

Some of the poetry in *Kalala Poems* previously appeared in literary publications such as *Blackfish*, *Tamarack Review*, *White Pelican*, *West Coast Review* and the *Capilano Review*. According to Kearns, Skyros Bruce travelled to India and afterwards spent time in several ashrams in British Columbia. She has returned to North Vancouver where she now works as a family counsellor and consultant among Aboriginal people, using a different name.

HENRY PENNIER

"Being a halfbreed, I had to fend for myself."—HENRY PENNIER

One of the first unfettered Aboriginal memoirs from British Columbia—not an extensively reworked "as told to" biography—is *Chiefly Indian: The Warm and Witty Story of a British Columbia Half Breed Logger* (1972) by Henry "Hank" Pennier.

Born in the Fraser Valley in 1904, Pennier was the grandson of a Quebec businessman who had arrived in British Columbia in the 1870s, then left his Aboriginal wife and their son George in order to return to Quebec. George Pennier grew up on a Harrison River homestead and married another halfbreed (Pennier's term and spelling) named Alice Davis. Two of their eight children died.

Not long after Henry Pennier was born, George Pennier died in a hunting accident in 1904. Growing up on an 87-acre homestead adjoining the Chehalis Reservation, Henry Pennier had a step-father from Union Bar, a settlement about three miles east of Hope, where he heard many Aboriginal stories from his step-grandfather.

Henry Pennier attended the St. Mary's mission school operated by the Oblates, becoming an altar boy. Forced to leave that school at age thirteen due to over-enrollment, he attended a public school at Hope until age fifteen. He started logging in 1922.

In 1924, Pennier married Margaret Leon, "a Harrison River Indian too except there is just a little Chinese in her." They had eight children: "And all of us are halfbreeds not white men and not Indian yet we look Indian and everybody but Indians takes us for Indians."

Pennier worked as a logger but suffered serious injuries that

Chiefly Indian
by HENRY PENNIER

The Warm and Witty Story of a British Columbia Half Breed Logger

edited by Herbert L. McDonald

left him reliant on a crutch and cane, and unemployable. Formerly active as a field lacrosse player, he used his sense of humour in his stories to become a raconteur and rustic philosopher. "About the only good thing about a being a halfbreed," he maintained, "[was] I could buy liquor."

In old age he was reduced to bingo, *Reader's Digest*, television and social assistance, but he retained his proud sense of accomplishment for having worked extremely hard for most of his years.

While he was living on Nicomen Trunk Road, east of Mission, Pennier received a visit from Welsh-born linguistics professor E. Wyn Roberts, who hoped to record some of Pennier's "Indian stories" on tape for an SFU linguistic project involving the Halkomelen language. Pennier was congenial but not easily controlled. Roberts soon discovered that Pennier basically wanted to tell his own stories instead.

After several meetings and textual collaborations, Roberts essentially abandoned his initial plans for his linguistic approach and decided to serve as Pennier's unofficial agent. Impressed by Pennier's intelligence and wit, Roberts approached Jack Richards, an editor at the *Vancouver Sun*, suggesting a weekly series featuring Henry Pennier's anecdotes and stories. Richards, in turn, connected the Roberts/Pennier duo with West Vancouver publisher and photographer Herb McDonald.

Chiefly Indian appeared when Hank Pennier was sixty-eight. Although it is highly amusing rather than sociological or literary,

Pennier's self-penned memoir, complete with some original spellings, concludes with some serious commentary about his halfbreed status.

"Outside of my work I could not join the white society, socially, and if I went to an Indian party and there was liquor involved I was taking a chance being jailed regardless of whether I had supplied them with liquor or not. If I had an Indian in the car and also a sealed bottle of whiskey or a sealed case of beer and a cop stops me on a routine check I would be charged with kniving [conniving] which has several meanings like the intention of giving him a drink sooner or later."

Pennier hopefully suggested that someday racial differentiations won't be made "but I know I won't be around then. Too bad because then there won't be any halfbreeds either and that will be a damn good thing."

CATHERINE BIRD

Yinka Déné is a term for the Athapascan-speaking people of northern British Columbia. The Yinka Déné Language Institute in Vanderhoof, founded in 1988, is devoted to the preservation and promotion of Yinka Déné language and culture. Catherine Bird, née Prince, also known as Catherine Coldwell, is a Nak'azdli band member who served as the Yinke Déné Language Institute's senior language instructor for its teacher training program. She started working on the Dakelh language with the Carrier Linguistic Committee in Fort Saint James in the 1960s.

After pioneering the introduction of Dakelh (Carrier) language instruction in public schools in northern B.C., Bird taught the language at the primary and secondary school levels and at the University of Northern British Columbia. From 1996 through 1999 she was the president of the Carrier Linguistic Committee.

Her children's books are *The Boy Who Snared the Sun* (1994) and *The Robin and the Song Sparrow* (1994). In addition, she co-authored the first modern Dakelh dictionary, *Central Carrier Bilingual Dictionary* (1974), a dictionary of the Nak'albun/Dzinghubun (Stuart/Trembleur Lake) dialect containing about three thousand entries. It was compiled by Francesca Antoine, Catherine Bird, Agnes Isaac, Nellie Prince, Sally Sam, Richard Walker and David B. Wilkinson.

DAN GEORGE

"This one Indian will not vanish from your memory."
—JUDITH CRIST, *NEW YORK TIMES*

Chief Dan George was born on July 24, 1899, on Burrard Reserve No. 3 in North Vancouver as the son of a chief of the Tsleil Waututh or Burrard band. He was given the name Tes-wah-no but was also known as Geswanouth Slahoot. In English he was Dan Slaholt. His surname was changed to George when he went to a mission boarding school at age five. There he was forbidden to speak his native language and was not allowed to practise Aboriginal traditions or beliefs.

Dan George left school at age seventeen and worked as a logger for three years and as a stevedore for 28 years. He stopped working as a longshoreman in 1947 after a large swingload of lumber smashed into him, damaging his leg and his hip. He then worked in construction and as a bus driver.

Dan George also formed a small dance band that entertained in clubs. He played the double bass and travelled to rodeos and country fairs in a group called Dan George and his Indian Entertainers. During this period he was elected Chief of His Reserve and served for 12 years in that capacity.

Chief Dan George at the Pacific National Exhibition in Vancouver

In the 1960s he was asked to audition for the role of "Old Antoine," in the CBC series *Cariboo Country* after the white actor playing the role fell seriously ill. Producer Philip Keatley needed a replacement within one week so Dan George was hired even though he was sixty years of age. To seal the deal, Keatley gave minor roles to Bob and Leonard George, the chief's two sons.

One episode of the series, entitled *How to Break a Quarterhorse,* won the Canadian Film Award for best entertainment film of 1965 and became the basis for a movie adaptation called *Smith,* starring Glen Ford and Keenan Wynn. In the final scene Dan George was called upon to deliver the speech of surrender given by Chief Joseph of the Nez Percé tribe of Idaho. During his audition, the cast of the movie was so impressed by his performance they formed a receiving line so everyone could shake his hand. One critic wrote that Dan George played the role to "ultimate perfection."

Dan George also gained widespread recognition for his performance in the original stage presentation of George Ryga's *The Ecstasy of Rita Joe* (Vancouver Playhouse, 1967). Another famous performance was his recitation of *A Lament for Confederation* before a crowd of 35,000 at Empire Stadium in Vancouver during centennial celebrations in 1967:

"How long have I known you, oh Canada? A hundred years? Yes, a hundred years. . . . I have seen my freedom disappear like the salmon going mysteriously out to sea. The white man's strange customs which I could not understand, pressed down upon me until I could no longer breathe.

"When I fought to protect my land and my home, I was called a savage. When I neither understood nor welcomed this way of life, I was called lazy. When I tried to rule my people, I was stripped of my authority.

"My nation was ignored in your history textbooks—they were little more important in the history of Canada than the buffalo that ranged the plains. I was ridiculed in your plays and motion pictures, when I drank your fire water, I got drunk—very, very drunk. And I forgot.

"Oh Canada, how can I celebrate with you this Centenary, this hundred years? Shall I thank you for the reserves that are left to me of my beautiful forests? For the canned fish of my rivers? For the loss of my pride and authority, even among my own people? For the lack of my will to fight back? No! I must forget what's past and gone.

"Oh, God in Heaven! . . . Like the Thunderbird of old I shall rise again out of the sea; I shall grab the instruments of the white man's success—his education, his skills, and with these new tools I shall build my race into the proudest segment of your society. Before I follow the great Chiefs who have gone before us, oh Canada, I shall see these things come to pass.

"I shall see our young braves and our chiefs sitting in the houses of law and government, ruling and being ruled by the knowledge and freedom of our great land. So shall we shatter the barriers of our isolation. So shall

Chief Dan George and Francis Hyland in The Ecstasy of Rita Joe, *1969*

the next hundred years be the greatest and proudest in the proud history of our tribes and nations."

At age seventy-one, Dan George was nominated for an Academy Award for Best Supporting Actor for his portrayal of a Cheyenne chief opposite Dustin Hoffman in *Little Big Man* (1970). He won the New York Film Critics Award and the National Society of Film Critics Award for that same role.

Starring with Frances Hyland, Dan George earned rave reviews for subsequent productions of *The Ecstasy of Rita Joe* at the National Arts Centre in Ottawa and in Washington, D.C.

In Washington, when he was approached by activists seeking to enlist his support for militant actions at Wounded Knee, South Dakota, in 1973, he responded, "We buried the hatchet in Canada long ago, and although treaty after treaty has been broken we have never dug it up. We have troubles, but we have our council of chiefs to work on them."

Other film appearances included playing elderly Indians in both *Harry and Tonto* (1974) and *The Outlaw Josey Wales* (1974) with Clint Eastwood. He also appeared in a forgettable and demeaning Bob Hope movie called *Cancel My Reservation*, for which he was criticized, and made guest appearances on TV shows such as *Incredible Hulk*, *Bonanza* and *The Beachcombers*.

He received an honorary Doctor of Laws degree from SFU in 1972 and from the University of Brandon in 1973. He died September 23, 1981. His grave alongside Dollarton Highway, in the burial compound on the Burrard Indian Reserve in North Vancouver, is not prominently marked.

Dan George is credited as the author of one of the bestselling books from B.C., *My Heart Soars* (1974), as well as the posthumous volumes, *My Spirit Soars* (1982) and *The Best of Chief Dan George* (2004). All three are collections of poetic oratory with illustrations by Mission artist Helmut Hirnschall.

According to Dan George's biographer Hilda Mortimer, who co-wrote *You Call Me Chief: Impressions of the Life of Chief Dan George* (1981), "Dan George's writing was not really his own. He had a mentor and a guide who dictated most of what he uttered. This was a very erudite and warm Catholic priest [Father Herbert 'Bert' Francis Dunlop, O.M.I.] who actually wrote most of what is in Dan George's books. It is ironic to remember Dan George as a writer because, of course, there was almost no tradition of that kind of literature for his generation at all."

His granddaughter Lee Maracle strongly rebuts Mortimer's claim and maintains Dan George directly narrated the words that appeared in print.

KENNETH B. HARRIS

In 1948 Arthur McDames was persuaded by his nephew Kenneth B. Harris to tape record Gitksan myths in his Tsomalia language. Harris provided translations of his uncle's stories into English via his mother Irene Harris, a woman in her eighties. These versions, in turn, were edited by Frances Robinson of the UBC Department of Fine Arts for *Visitors Who Never Left: The Origin of the People of Damelahamid* (1974). In addition to tracing the ancient history of the people who live between the Skeena and Nass rivers, Harris' account recalls the origins of the Killer Whale and Thunderbird, Twtjea-adku, as well as the revenge of Medeek, the bear who arose from a lake to punish people for their misdeeds. According to Robinson, the stories "have not been tampered with in any way and are given exactly as translated by Ken Harris, using his own divisions and order." Arguably, these stories can be credited as much to McDames. Harris inherited McDames' title Hagbegwatku, meaning "first-born of the nation."

VERNA KIRKNESS

Born in 1935 on the Fisher River Reserve in Manitoba, Verna Kirkness of the Cree Nation became the founding director of the First Nations House of Learning at the University of British Columbia in 1987.

Kirkness spearheaded the creation of the First Nations Longhouse, a 2,000-square-meter educational facility that serves as a "home away from home" for Aboriginal students. This magnificent building made of West Coast cedar and copper roofing imported from France officially opened on May 25, 1993.

Kirkness began her teaching career at age eighteen and held positions as principal, education counsellor, supervisor of schools, curriculum consultant and education director for the Manitoba Indian Brotherhood (Assembly of Manitoba Chiefs) and the National Indian Brotherhood (Assembly of First Nations) before she came to British Columbia to work as the Supervisor of the Native Indian Teacher Education Program and Director of Indian Education at UBC.

Kirkness co-authored *Khot-La Cha: An Autobiography of Chief Simon Baker* (1994), with Simon Baker, as well as *The First Nations Longhouse, Our Home Away from Home* (2001), with Jo-ann Archibald.

She also self-published *Aboriginal Languages: A Collection of Talks and Papers* (1998) and co-edited a resource book with D. Bruce Sealey, entitled *Indians Without Tipis* (1973). Her other titles are *Indians of the Plains* (1984) and *First Nations and Schools* (1992).

For her work as an administrator, educator and author, Verna Kirkness received the Order of Canada, as well as honorary degrees from Mount St. Vincent University, the University of Western Ontario and the University of British Columbia.

Kirkness retired to live in Winnipeg. "Education has been my whole life," she says.

Verna Kirkness at UBC, 1994

GEORGE MANUEL

"The thing that I remember of my life,
our lives I should say, is the poverty."—GEORGE MANUEL

The best-known Aboriginal from modern British Columbia has been Chief Dan George but possibly the most important has been political organizer George Manuel. He was president of the National Indian Brotherhood (1970–1976), president of the Union of British Columbia Indian Chiefs (1979–1981), and first president of the World Council of Indigenous Peoples (1975–1981).

With Michael Posluns, Manuel co-authored *The Fourth Way: An Indian Reality* (1974), which promoted the concept and rights of indigenous peoples. To spread his message of unification for indigenous peoples, Manuel travelled extensively througout Central and South America, the United States and Europe.

In the late 1970s he made a speech to 15,000 indigenous Peruvians. "I told them that we have to have our own ideology," he said. "We don't fit into the Right and we don't fit

George Manuel

into the Left. That's why we are fragmented completely; we are always on the losing end, the deprived end of the stick. That was the first time an ideal was ever proclaimed in Native culture. Now that the idea has come it's talked about in many parts of the world, but there is no movement, just talk. I'm proud that I introduced the idea."

Born on February 21, 1921, on Neskonlith Reserve within Shuswap (Secwepemc) territory in the B.C. interior, George Manuel was raised by his grandparents and attended Kamloops Residential School until he contracted tuberculosis at age twelve. He was confined to a sanatorium and never fully recovered from the humiliating experience. Mainly self-educated, he worked as a busboy, fruit picker, logger and boom boss in the forest industry.

With guidance from his mentor in politics, North Vancouver's Andrew Paull (subject of a little-known biography by Herbert Francis Dunlop), George Manuel served for seven years as chief of the Shuswap and became president of the North American Indian Brotherhood of B.C. in 1959.

In an effort to speed the process of reform and self-determination, Manuel took a position within the Department of Indian Affairs but became radicalized in opposition to the government when Prime Minister Pierre Trudeau issued the White Paper in 1969 that announced Canada's intention to dissolve Indian nations and promote the "assimilation of Indian people into Canadian society."

To mobilize against the Trudeau plan, Manuel got himself elected as president of the National Indian Brotherhood. During this period of radicalization he was inspired and influenced by his personal audience with Julius Nyerere in Tanzania and a visit to the Maoris of New Zealand in 1971.

Manuel also went to Washington, D.C., to contact his counterpart in the

Andrew Paull

United States, Mel Tonasket, president of the National Congress of American Indians. This meeting led to an international agreement in 1973 to establish exchanges between the two Aboriginal associations, thereby laying the groundwork for affiliations between indigenous peoples around the world.

George Manuel was also instrumental in drafting the Universal Declaration of the Rights of Indigenous Peoples and in developing the Union of B.C. Indian Chiefs' Aboriginal Rights Position Paper. As well, he contributed to numerous position papers, including *Evaluation of Indian Education* (1967), *Indian Economic Development: A Whiteman's Whitewash* (1972), *National Indian Brotherhood on Department of Indian and Northern Affairs Guidelines* (1975), *Indian Sovereignty: The Indian Bible of British Columbia* (1977) and *Report on the World Council of Indigenous Peoples* (1977).

George Manuel died in Kamloops on November 15, 1989. His son, Bob Manuel (1948–1998), led the Union of B.C. Indian Chiefs during the early 1980s.

LEE MARACLE

"White men have become the rootless, the lost, and the ridiculous. . . .
I am no longer on the periphery of their world and cut off from mine;
they are on the periphery of mine." —NARRATOR, *SUNDOGS*

Lee Maracle, of Salish and Cree ancestry, is a member of the Stó:lo First Nation and one of the first Aboriginal writers in Canada to publish fiction. Her ground-breaking synthesis of autobiography and fiction, *Bobbi Lee, Indian Rebel* (1975), recounts travels in the 1960s and 1970s within B.C., California and Toronto's counter-cultural community. It admonishes the rest of Canada to "search out the meaning of colonial robbery and figure out how you are going to undo it all."

Published twelve years later, *I Am Woman* (1988) describes Maracle's struggle to "climb the mountain of racism." Including poetry and photos of loved ones, *I Am Woman* was first published by her second husband Dennis Maracle, who also helped Maracle publish a collection of poems, *Seeds*.

In *Sundogs* (1992), promoted as Lee Maracle's first novel, a twenty-year-old East Vancouver sociology student, Marianne, wants relief from her mother's railings at the television news and insistence that white society is an anti-Native genocidal plot. As the only unilingual sibling of five, Marianne lacks confidence in Aboriginal ways. Beset by family upheavals, racism and patriarchy, she feels "tethered to the hot wire of my own rage."

Over the course of one summer in *Sundogs*, Marianne is liberated by Elijah Harper's anti-constitutional stance and the Oka stand-off. "If Elijah upset Canada, he upset me more. His message to us was profoundly simple; we are worth fighting for, we are worth caring for, we are worthy." Marianne has an affair with her boss, an Aboriginal rights lobbyist, but rejects him when she learns he is married. She joins a First Nations long distance run from Penticton to Oka, carrying a feather for peace. She also feels inspired by sundogs, "impossible images reflected under extraordinary circumstances."

In Maracle's novel, *Ravensong* (1993), urban Aboriginal women in a Pacific Northwest community that is beset by a flu epidemic in the 1950s must choose between saving the lives of elders or the lives of their babies. The young protagonist, Stacey, is at odds with her mother's adherence to old customs. Circling and touching the storyline are Raven's musings, which poke fun and impart wisdom.

Maracle's first young adult novel, *Will's Garden* (2002), describes the ceremonial traditions of Stó:lo boys who are becoming men.

"I was born in Vancouver on July 2nd 1950 and raised on the North Shore mud flats about two miles east of Second Narrows Bridge," Maracle writes in her first book. At fourteen, she became one of B.C.'s top high school long-distance runners. Maracle attended Simon Fraser University and became a member of the

A former long distance runner, Lee Maracle is entering her fourth decade as an author.

Red Power Movement and Liberation Support Movement. A recipient of the Before Columbus American Book Award, she has worked at the Barrie Native Friendship Centre in Ontario, performed on stage and taught courses at the University of Toronto and taught at Western Washington University in Bellingham, Washington. She has since returned to Ontario to teach.

In 1990, Maracle's monograph from Gallerie Publications explained her resistance to European academic models. That same year she co-edited the proceedings of a 1988 conference, *Telling It: Women and Language Across Cultures* (1994) and released her first compilation of stories, *Sojourner's Truth* (1992). Her 1992 essay for Vancouver's *Step* magazine entitled "Goodbye Columbus" recalls that her Métis mother worked up to 16 hours a day at physical labour to feed and clothe her seven children.

Maracle is also the author of *Sojourners & Sundogs* (1999), *Bent Box* (2000) and *Daughters Are Forever* (2002). She has co-authored/edited *Telling It: Women and Language Across Cultures* (1994), *Reconciliation: The En'owkin Journal of First North American Peoples*

(2002), *My Home As I Remember* (1998) and *We Get Our Living Like Milk from the Land* (1993–94).

"We're socially locked in time," she told *Redwire* magazine in 2003. "If we are burning sage or saying million-year-old prayers, then we are OK; as long as we are back in the bush or spiritual mode we're safe. If we're doing anything else people want to erase us, they want to not see us. So my stories, I think, allow people to see us in a myriad of circumstances and once people see us differently they might hear us differently as well."

BERNADETTE ROSETTI

Born in 1912, the late Bernadette Rosetti prepared a genealogical study of the descendants of Chief Kwah, her great-grandfather, in Carrier, with an English translation, photographs and charts for *Kw'eh Ts'u Haindene: Descendants of Kwah – A Carrier Indian Genealogy* (1979).

Also known as Chief Kw'eh (c. 1755–1840), Kwah welcomed Simon Fraser when his people guided the explorer to Tsaooche village in Sowchea Bay. Simon Fraser presented Kwah with a red cloth that one of Kwah's descendants provided to the government of Canada in 1997. It was also Chief Kwah who once took Hudson's Bay Company trader James Douglas as his prisoner during a disagreement in 1828, never to be forgotten by Douglas. This incident is described in the memoirs of William Henry Pierce.

Burial monument for Chief Kwah

Bernadette Rosetti also published an undated, spiral-bound children's story entitled *Nunulk'i'-un* and she retold a traditional story with many known variants in Nak'albun dialect for *Musdzi 'Udada'/The Owl Story: A Carrier Indian Legend* (1991), with an English translation. In the story, a young boy, repeatedly warned to go to bed, refuses and is snatched by an owl that carries him away to her nest. The boy is fed and nurtured by the owl while his father searches for him, asking squirrel, rabbit and grouse for assistance. Finally the hen, in exchange for having her eyelids painted red, directs the father to the tree where the owl has her nest. Edited by Edward John, the children's book was illustrated by Roman Muntener.

DAISY SEWID-SMITH

Daughter of James Sewid, Daisy Sewid-Smith is an expert on the history of her Kwakwaka'wakw people. As a linguist teaching for the University of Victoria in Campbell River, she translated the memoirs of her grandmother Agnes Alfred (c.1890–1992), a non-literate storyteller and historian, for *Paddling to Where I Stand: Agnes Alfred, Qwiqwasutinuxw Noblewoman* (2004), the first biographical portrayal of a Kwakwaka'wakw matriarch.

She also wrote *Prosecution or Persecution* (1979) to document the enforcement of the law forbidding the potlatch as of 1884. In particular she records the actions of Indian agent William Halliday who confiscated Kwakiutl property between 1913 and 1932. Halliday wrote, "The law against the potlatch has been passed because it has been seen that where the potlatch exists there has been no progress and the Government wants to see the Indians advance so that they are on the same footing as the white men, and this can not be as long as the potlatch continues."

Asked to do a booklet pertaining to the imprisonments and

the confiscation of masks and coppers, in conjuction with the opening of the Cape Mudge Museum on Quadra Island, Sewid-Smith realized the need to produce *Prosecution or Persecution.*

"For many years I have had in my possession tape recordings of the imprisonments and other historical data," she wrote. "It was with this information and other information acquired through research that the booklet was started. We soon realized that a booklet would not be sufficient to tell our history and it had to be told in order to show why our Ba-

Daisy Sewid-Smith

sah [potlatch] was outlawed. This book, therefore, is just a memorial to those who gave so much of themselves in preserving our history before the coming of the white man and what happened after their arrival."

Daisy Sewid-Smith lives in Campbell River.

PHYLLIS CHELSEA

A long with her husband Chief Andy Chelsea, Phyllis Chelsea led a movement during the 1970s to abstain from alcohol and drugs within the Alkali Lake Indian Band, now known as the Esketemc, a nation of approximately 600 Secwepemc (Shuswap) people south of Williams Lake. At one time the Alkali Band had an alcoholism rate estimated as high as 100 percent. The social devastation caused primarily by substance abuse was such that others referred to the community as Alcohol Lake. Liquor stores and taxis in Williams Lake benefited from the widespread, chronic addiction. There were regular deliveries three times per week on the so-called "Dog Creek Stage," and bootlegging was rampant.

Phyllis Chelsea was the first to abstain, followed by her husband four days later, in June of 1972. They were responding to their seven-year-old daughter Ivy who told them, "I don't want to live with you anymore." The Chelsea family was encouraged by Alcoholics Anonymous counsellor Ed Lynch, an Oblate Brother.

Andy Chelsea was elected as band chief soon after he quit drinking. He instituted a variety of reforms, some of which were very unpopular, in order to achieve an abstention rate of more than 90 percent by 1979. Liquor sales on the reserve were banned, the RCMP used marked bills to entrap local bootleggers (including the mothers of Andy and Phyllis Chelsea), chronic drinkers received vouchers for Williams Lake stores instead of welfare money, an alcoholic priest was encouraged to leave the reserve and perpetrators of alcohol-related crimes were given the choice between

VICKIE JENSEN PHOTO

Phyllis Chelsea

jail and undergoing treatment.

Ivy Chelsea, a single mother of five, is now employed as a Secwepemc teacher and a facilitator and trainer for Letwilc Trainings. Sometimes accompanied by her mother, Ivy Chelsea has travelled extensively to Aboriginal communities, sharing the story of her people's progress. Andy and Phyllis Chelsea made similar trips for years across North America and Australia, recalling their experiences. Their inspirational story of attempting to "dry out" the Alkali Lake Band has been recorded in a documentary film, *Honor of All: The Story of Alkali Lake*, that was released in 1986.

The first Aboriginal to be elected to the Cariboo Chilcotin School Board, Phyllis Chelsea has received the Order of Canada, the Order of British Columbia and an honorary degree from UBC for her work. She has been instrumental in revitalizing Shuswap language and culture within schools, co-authoring *Learning Shuswap, Books 1–2* (1980).

CHARLES JONES

"I can name seven generations back in our family."
—CHIEF CHARLES JONES

Charlie Jones' co-written memoir *Queesto, Pacheenaht Chief by Birthright* (1981) is one of four titles that launched Theytus Books. It provides a rare, first-hand account of Aboriginal life on Vancouver Island in the nineteenth century.

Chief Charles Jones of the Pacheenaht tribe of the Nuu-chah-nulth First Nation was born on July 7, 1876. As a boy of six or seven, he began attending the missionary school at Clo-oose where they changed his name from Queesto to Jones. He first used a Winchester .44 at age nine and began hunting for game at age

Methodist-run Coqualeetza School, near Chilliwack, operated from 1880 until World War II. These students attended around 1890, shortly after Charlie Jones was a student.

ten. After two years at a nearby school at Neah Bay, he was sent to the Coqualeetza Residential School in the Fraser Valley, travelling from New Westminster to Chilliwack on the *Beaver*, the Hudson's Bay Company boat. He stayed at Sardis among 189 students for two years until he quit around age twelve. The food was bad, the Coqualeetza teachers had arbitrarily put him back three grades, and the students were forced to do farm labour.

"In those days," he claimed, "Indians could only go as far as Grade Eight in the residential schools anyway, and that's not enough education. That was what they did to the Indians in those days—they wouldn't let them get past Grade Eight." The government had legislated mandatory school attendance in 1884.

In 1900 Jones worked for four months as a traditional pelagic seal hunter in the Bering Sea, harpooning seals from a dugout canoe for the Victoria Sealing Company. He came home with $1,000.

Charlie Jones became chief of his tribe in 1921. That same year, after two years of planning, he held his first potlatch for eight days, building a new longhouse for the occasion. Jones' appreciation of his Aboriginal heritage was ingrained, partly from a grandfather who had owned many slaves, had hunted whales with a harpoon, and had eight potlatches in his lifetime, but also from his father, who raised him in a traditional Pacheenaht longhouse. The family travelled extensively in their 60-foot canoe and made money catching sea otters. "You could go right around Vancouver Island with a canoe if you carried enough food," Jones wrote. He claimed his father once loaned money to the Hudson's Bay Company when their trading post went broke. "The manager of the trading post in Victoria, a man named Jack Godman," Jones recalled, "asked my father if he could borrow $5,000. So my father lent him the money, and within seven months the Hudson's Bay Company paid him back the $5,000 with another $200 for interest."

For about 50 years, Charlie Jones worked in many parts of the logging industry and later owned and operated his own fishing boat, the *Queesto*. In retirement he took up carving dugout canoes and masks. In 1974, at the request of the Provincial Museum, he made a six-man canoe.

Charles Jones

Before he died in 1983, at age one hundred and seven, Jones co-wrote his memoir *Queesto,* with Stephen Bosustow, a Hollywood animator and film producer born in Victoria. Bosustow first came to the Pacheenaht Reservation near Port Renfrew in July of 1976 in order to visit his cousin, Roberta Bosustow Jones, who had married Charles Jones, Jr., son of Chief Charlie Jones. The Chief had just celebrated his 100th birthday earlier that same month. "The name of my family is Queesto," Jones told Bosustow, "a name which means Chief of Chief over all Chiefs."

Along with the memoirs of Charlie Nowell and Hank Pennier, *Queesto* is an exceptionally readable account that has not been unduly filtered, and Jones' longevity makes it particularly valuable. He recalls nineteenth-century childhood games, slavery, the coming of Christianity, hunting and fishing methods, foods gathered from nature, folk stories, potlatches and other customs.

"The white man buries his dead in the ground," Jones explains, "while the Indian puts the body up in a tree. The white man could never understand why we did this. The old people didn't think that there was any use in telling them that if they buried their dead in the ground, the wolves would get the scent, dig the body up and eat it. Even if the dead person was put in a coffin, the wolves would dig the whole coffin up and break up the wood. . . . So that's why we put our dead up in the trees instead of burying them—there was no religious reason, it was just to keep them out of reach of the wolves."

LUKE SWAN

As a commercial fisherman, David William Ellis became acquainted with Aboriginal elders Luke Swan of Ahousat and Solomon Wilson of Skidegate and recorded their memories and knowledge of how Aboriginals have used the intertidal zones. Ellis subsequently co-authored *Teachings of the Tides: Uses of Marine Invertebrates by the Manhousat People* (1981) with Luke Francis Swan, also known as Tl'itl'iits-sulh, meaning "arrow in the eye." George Louie, Sr., of Victoria served as a liaison between Ellis and Swan, who began sharing information on their subject in 1974. Wayne Campbell and Nancy J. Turner provided assistance with scientific identification of species. Born in 1893, Luke Swan was still fishing and being asked to sing and compose songs for potlatches in 1981, the year *Teachings of the Tides* became one of the first four titles from Theytus Books. It concludes with a brief chapter on supernatural creatures or sea serpents.

"Mr. Swan's father came upon one when he and another man were hunting for sea otter near Hesquiat Point. He shot an arrow at it, but missed. . . . Mr. Swan's father watched the beast crawl onto a beach and disappear into the forest. If he had succeeded in killing it, he would have become a very great man, for nobody ever killed a sea serpent on the west coast of Vancouver Island."

——◦◦◦◦——

JAMES WALLAS

"Today you get in your car and go to the store—it was canoe in them days." —CHIEF JAMES WALLAS

Born at Bear Cove, the original site of Port Hardy, on March 15, 1907, Chief James Wallas was also known as "J.J." or Jimmy Jumbo, like his father, who was from the Quatsino tribe on Quatsino Sound. His mother, Jeanny Jumbo, was from Hope Island, where James Wallas spent his summers. At age nineteen, Wallas married Annie Charlie from Village Harbour and soon began working on fishing boats, eventually becoming the skipper of a seine boat. During World War II he was a foreman at the Port Alice pulp mill, in charge of 32 men. Wallas also fished for halibut and completed an Indian Education Teachers' Training program in Campbell River to teach Indian Studies. He taught Indian Studies at Coal Harbour after the people from his old village at Quatsino had moved there to be closer to schools and medical services.

Growing up mainly on Quatsino Sound, Wallas learned traditional stories from elders, mostly from his father's brother, for

Chief James Wallas

Kwakiutl Legends (1981), as told to Pamela Whitaker. "Usually four families would share a longhouse," he recalled, "one in each corner, each having their own fire. If only two families were in a dwelling they would often share a fire." One of his stories concerns the trickster-like character of the Mink, lewd and handsome, who must go through a succession of wives (Kelp, Frog, Boulder and Cloud) before he is finally content with Lizard. Another story concerns Mink's efforts to come to terms with manhood. In Kwak'wala, Mink can be translated as "Made-Like-The-Sun" because Mink believes he is the son of the Sun. Wallas' collection of Kwakiutl origin stories, animal stories and recollections of whaling are complemented by "prayers" taken from Franz Boas' *The Religion of the Kwakiutl Indians, Part II–Translations* (1930) as well as a brief appendix prepared by linguist Peter J. Wilson who was involved in the initial efforts to introduce Kwak'wala language programs on Vancouver Island.

ELLEN WHITE

In addition to *Queesto, Teachings of the Tides* and a reprint of *Gone Indian*, a novel by non-Aboriginal Robert Kroetsch, one of the first four titles from Theytus Books was Ellen White's first reader for children, *Kwulasulwut: Stories from the Coast Salish* (1981), illustrated by David Neel. Two of the stories in the collection are "Father Barbeques," in which a child instructs his father how to

Ellen White assisted in midwifery at age nine and began delivering babies at age sixteen.

cook, and "The Stolen Sun," in which Raven and Sea Urchin must work together to free the Sun after it has been captured by Seagull.

White's follow-up is *Kwulasulwut II* (1997), featuring four more English versions of Salish legends adapted for children, with colour illustrations by Okanagan band member and teacher Bill Cohen. The supernatural adventure tales are "The Mink and the Raccoon Family," "Smuy the Little Deer," "Deer, Raven and the Red Snow," and "Journey to the Moon."

Growing up on Rice (Norway) Island, White was taught Coast Salish cultural information, including hunting and fishing, by her grandparents and her parents Charles and Hilda Rice. She married Doug White and moved to Nanaimo where she raised her children in the Nanaimo Nation. As a storyteller and medicine woman of the Snuneymuxw First Nation, she has been Elder-in-Residence at Malaspina College in Nanaimo. Her Aboriginal name Kwulasulwut means "many stars."

II
SEEING RED

Jeannette Armstrong was a negotiator during the Gustafsen Lake stand-off in 1995.

JEANNETTE ARMSTRONG

*"The role I have in my family is as an archivist, recorder
of history and knowledge-keeper."* —JEANNETTE ARMSTRONG

Now the most influential figure in the Aboriginal writing community, Jeannette Armstrong made her literary debut at age fifteen when she published a poem about John F. Kennedy in the local newspaper.

"The process of writing as a Native person," says Armstrong, born on the Penticton Indian Reservation in 1948, "has been a healing one for me because I've uncovered the fact that I'm not a savage, not dirty and ugly and not less because I have brown skin, or a Native philosophy."

Influenced by the cadence of Pauline Johnson's poetry, the mentoring of Okanagan storyteller Harry Robinson and Summerland-based playwright and novelist George Ryga, Jeannette Armstong then released a slim story for young readers, *Walk in Water* (1982), about two girls named Neekna and Chemia who grow up in the Okanagan Valley before the coming of the white man.

Seven years later, in conjunction with Theytus Books and the En'owkin Centre in Pentiction, Armstrong oversaw the creation of the En'owkin International School of Writing for Native Students in conjunction with the University of Victoria's Bachelor of Fine Arts Program and Okanagan College, a focal point for Aboriginal writing throughout North America.

Today Armstrong is widely known for her novel *Slash* (1983), reprinted nine times and frequently adopted for use in schools. It records alienation and militancy during the period from 1960 to 1983. Despite some ridicule from friends, its protagonist Thomas Kelasket enjoys speaking the Okanagan language and attending powwows, but eventually he's forced to confront racism in a white-operated school. Sometimes angry and confused, he travels widely in North America to come to terms with himself and the world.

Although *Slash* features a male protagonist, its plot is not without some similarities to Armstrong's own trajectory as an artist and organizer. Her *Whispering in Shadows* (2000) can be read as a companion novel to *Slash*. It follows the life and times of Penny, an Okanagan artist and single mother who has contracted cancer after her exposure to pesticides while working as a fruit picker in the Okanagan Valley. An environmental activist, she travels the world in support of other indigenous cultures, gradually developing her own political and social theories. While beset by "globalization and supremacy deceit and grudging paternalism," Penny ultimately comes to accept her place in the universe, comforted to know she will be returned to the earth when she dies.

Armstrong's best-known non-fiction book is *Native Creative Process* (1991), in collaboration with Aboriginal architect Douglas Cardinal. She has edited, or contributed to, numerous collaborative books that include *This is a Story, All My Relations: An Anthology of Contemporary Canadian Native Fiction* (1990); *Aboriginal Perspectives of the Natural Environment* (1991); *Give Back: First Nations Perspectives on Cultural Practice* (1992); *We Get Our Living Like*

Milk from the Land (1993); and *Looking at the Words of Our People: First Nations Analysis of Literature* (1993). Her other titles are *Neekna & Chemai* (1984), *Breath Tracks* (1991), *Dancing with the Cranes* (2004) and an audio book entitled *Grandmothers* (1995).

Jeannette Armstrong earned her Bachelor of Fine Arts from the University of Victoria in 1978. A documentary film portrait, *Jeannette Armstrong: Knowledge-Keeper*, was produced by A.R.T.

BookWorld Productions and premiered on CBC in 1995. She received the Mungo Martin Award in 1974, the Helen Pitt Memorial Award in 1978, an Honorary Doctorate of Letters from St. Thomas University in 2000 and the Buffett Award for Indigenous Leadership in 2003.

Fluent in the Okanagan language, Armstrong recognizes the importance of her mother's great-aunt, the novelist Mourning Dove, who once lived in nearby Oliver, B.C., and taught Armstrong's mother in school. Armstrong grew up hearing first-hand stories about Mourning Dove, who died in 1936, twelve years before Armstrong's birth. "Reading her stories had a great influence on me," she says. "And I was really fortunate to have two grandmothers alive until I was well into my 20s."

FLORENCE DAVIDSON

Born in Masset on September 15, 1896, Florence Edenshaw Davidson was one of the most influential and best-known female elders of the Haida. She was born on the north end of Graham Island in Old Masset before present-day Masset was established in 1907. Related to renowned Haida artists Charles Edenshaw and Albert Edward Edenshaw, she was married at age fourteen to logger, fisherman, trapper and carver Robert Davidson, Sr., a hereditary chief of the town of Kayung.

They had 13 children including Claude Davidson, himself a carver and the chief of the village of Masset, who, in turn influenced the careers of her grandsons Robert Davidson and Reg Davidson, who trained under Bill Reid. The great-grandfather of Robert and Reg Davidson was Charles Edenshaw, Florence Edenshaw Davidson's father.

Florence Davidson has been credited with reviving the tradition of making button blankets among the Haida. She made her first button blanket in 1952 to console herself after her family lost their possessions in a house fire. She also made traditional woven baskets and hats.

As a revered conduit for her Haida culture, Davidson frequently collaborated with ethnologists, filmmakers and anthropologists such as Margaret Blackman, co-author of *During My Time: Florence Edenshaw Davidson, A Haida Woman* (1982).

Having been one of the last Haida women to undergo the traditional puberty seclusion and an arranged marriage, Davidson provided

Florence Davidson and her husband Robert, 1961

her biographer with keen appreciations of female roles in Haida society, including revelations about menopause and widowhood, derived from approximately 50 hours of tape recordings. A revised, enlarged edition appeared in 1992.

Partially as a tribute to Florence Davidson and other elders, Nancy J. Turner completed *Plants of Haida Gwaii* (2004), an ethnobotanical study of the Queen Charlotte Islands that Turner began with her first visit to Haida Gwaii in the early 1970s. Some of Nancy Turner's information on plants was gleaned directly from Florence Davidson, who invited her to attend her ninety-fifth birthday celebrations. Florence Davidson is depicted on the cover of the book in a photograph by Robert D. Turner showing her removing cedar bark from a red cedar in preparation for weaving. Florence Davidson, who greeted Queen Elizabeth at Sandspit in 1971, died in Masset in December of 1993.

SIMON WALKUS, SR.

A year before he died, Chief Simon Walkus, Sr., orally recorded his people's traditional stories in 1968 with Susanne Hilton, employed by the British Columbia Indian Advisory Committee, for possible use in local schools. These texts were translated by his daughter Evelyn Walkus Windsor of the Heiltsuk Cultural Education Centre in Bella Bella, with the assistance of Heiltsuk linguist John Rath, for *Oowekeeno Oral Traditions as Told by the Late Chief Simon Walkus, Sr.* (1982). The bilingual result is sometimes credited to Chief Walkus' daughter.

Oowekeeno Oral Traditions contains twelve stories and three songs in the Oowekyala Wakashan language, with interlinear English translation and explanations, to illustrate the relations of the Oowekeeno people to the natural and supernatural worlds. Heiltsuk (Bella Bella) and Oowekeeno (Owikyala) are considered to be dialects of the same language. The stories arose from the Rivers Inlet, a 48-kilometre inlet southwest of Bella Coola where Simon Walkus, Sr., was the second-eldest son of Chief Charles Walkus, Sr., of the Wannock River people, and where he and his wife Lila were both members of secret societies.

Simon Walkus, Sr., died in Rivers Inlet Village in 1969, aged approximately seventy-seven. The Walkus family has remained prominent in the tiny Oweekeno First Nation that shares territory with the Heiltsuk, Gwa'Sala-Nakwaxda'xw on the central B.C. coast. With 207 members, it formally applied to the B.C. Treaty Commission in 1993.

PETER S. WEBSTER

Born at Bear River (now called Bedwell River), in Clayoquot Sound on October 3, 1908, Peter Webster overcame frustration, prejudice, alcoholism and poverty to attain a degree in linguistics from the University of Victoria while in his seventies. "I don't think I had any shoes," he once recalled. "There were no shoes, no pants. I don't know what I wore before I got to know that I was in the world."

Webster's formal education within classrooms was limited to two years at the Ahousat School on Meares Island. "I didn't even know how to say 'yes,'" he later wrote, "and I used to get kicked or slapped or sent to bed without supper if the staff heard me use my own language." His schooling ended with an unhappy, forced marriage due to an unplanned pregnancy.

At age twenty, Peter Webster married his second wife Jessie, who became known as a maker of cedar hats. Once arrested for possession of the fur of seals, then arrested and sent to Oakalla prison for refusing to pay the provincial seine boat tax, Webster became known as a singer and a collector of songs and Ahousat lore, but he was plagued by alcoholism.

AS FAR AS I KNOW
Reminiscences of an Ahousat Elder

PETER S. WEBSTER
Illustrated by Kwayatsapalth

"The death of my oldest son, Basil Webster . . . marked the point when I started to live in the world again. . . . The step-brother of my wife, Jessie, came to me and told me plainly that because of my heavy drinking I was blind, deaf and senseless. I was not myself. This woke me up."

After Webster and his wife were featured in Ulli Steltzer's photography book *Indian Artists at Work* in 1976, Webster recorded his versions of Nuu-chah-nulth songs and at age seventy he dictated an autobiography, *As Far As I Know: Reminiscences of an Ahousat Elder* (1983), illustrated by his nephew Ron Hamilton (Kwayatsapalth). The final third of the book contains his versions of Ahousat stories and history, including their war with the Oo-tsus-aht in the 1840s or 1850s as recalled by his grandfather. Peter Webster's Nuu-chah-nulth name, O-Wo-Me-Yis, means Leader on the Beach.

STAN DIXON

"Why should the government be paying us welfare to do nothing when they could be paying us the same money under different legislative wording that would bring pride back to our people?"—STAN DIXON

First elected as Chief of the Sechelt Indian Band in 1983, Stan Dixon laid the groundwork for local Aboriginal self-government, which was formally achieved in Sechelt in 1986—the year he failed to gain re-election. His privately published memoir of those turbulent times is *Self-Government, A Spirit Reborn* (1986).

The Sechelt Indian Government District operates under some sections of British Columbia's Municipal Act but it is not required, like other municipalities, to hold open meetings. Stan Dixon alleged a lack of openness for the self-government of the Shishalh Nation that has slightly more than one thousand members.

Born in 1942 as a member of the Sechelt Nation, Hunaechin tribe, Wolf Clan, Dixon attended St. Augustine School in Sechelt and St. Mary's Residential School in Mission. He graduated from St. Thomas Aquinas High School in North Vancouver as one of

Stan Dixon

its first Aboriginal students. After working in the logging industry for 25 years, he was elected as a councillor of the Sechelt First Nation in 1972.

In 1992 he acquired proprietorship of the Aboriginal newspaper *Kahtou* and moved its headquarters to Sechelt. In 1993, Dixon was elected again as a Councillor to the District of Sechelt, and has been re-elected several times since.

A strong believer in private enterprise, he continued publishing *Kahtou* for more than ten years without a loan or grant. "The problem with grants," he said, "is all that paperwork. And things take too long. Business is like fishing. You have to be there when the fish are running. . . . Successful aboriginal entrepreneurs are those who advertise themselves. These are the people who'll turn a profit."

RICHARD MALLOWAY

According to ethnologist Brian Thom, Stó:lo Chief Richard Malloway (Th'eláchiyatel) was considered a direct descendant of the four original ancestors of the Chilliwacks: Th'eláchiyatel, Yexwpílem, Siyemchess, and X̱wexwayleq. He lived in the Lower Fraser Valley from 1907 to 1987. Fluent in English and Halq'eméylem, Malloway was selected in 1932 by Chief Billy Sepass of Skowkale, Chief Albert Douglas of Tzeachten and Chief Albert Louis of Yakweakwioose to serve as the spokesperson for those three bands. In the early 1940s he became chief of Yakweakwioose.

Malloway was one of the originators of the Cultus Lake Indian Festival at which he served as Master of Ceremonies. Shortly before he died in 1987, Malloway recorded an undated version of the Sxwayxwey story, with the assistance of Norman Todd, a local medical doctor. Malloway's storytelling has been distributed through the Coqualeetza Cultural Centre as part of *Telling Stories: The Life of Chief Richard Malloway* (1994), compiled by Thom with stories narrated by Mrs. Edna Malloway, Chief Frank Malloway and Chief Richard Malloway (1994).

Born in Sardis, B.C., on December 15, 1907, Malloway did not attend residential school due to illness. As a result, he was raised by his parents Julius and Mary Malloway, as well as by a shxwlá:m or medicine man named Catholic Tommy, who taught him to be a healer. Malloway was revered among the Stó:lo for his generosity and for maintaining winter spirit dancing during several decades when it was outlawed within the restrictions of the anti-Potlatch legislation.

Along with Charlie Douglas, Albert Nelson, Freddy Cheer, Aggie Victor, and Maggie Pennier, Malloway secretly held the winter dances on reserves, including the Sxwayxwey dance that could be performed only by members of the extended family of someone who "owned" the Sxwayxwey story. Although Malloway had received the story from his mother, he never himself used the Sxwayxwey mask in a dance.

Richard Malloway said, "My mother was born in Chilliwack, on the Skaw reserve in 1876, and this is her story — the Chilliwack story. I know the song of the Sxwayxwey and I recorded it. It says that the brother has a stomach of stone. That means that he is unfriendly and nobody likes him, and he doesn't like women. We are trying to revive the Sxwayxwey here, and, you know the rules of the Indians are strict. You have to belong to the family which found the mask if you want to use it. This is one of the reasons I want to record this. Since the mask came up here to my family we have the right to use it."

The story goes that two young girls from Harrison Mills caught the Sxwayxwey when they were fishing near the mouth of the Chehalis and Fraser Rivers. This creature had four spinners that were spinning as they pulled the Sxwayxwey out of the water. The

Sxwayxwey escaped back into the water but they were left with the Sxwayxwey mask and spinners.

The spinners were affixed to a band at the top of the mask. They gave the mask to their brother. Once, when he was being pursued by a different tribe, he jumped into the water. The feathered headband he was wearing came off his head and it floated down the river, serving as a decoy. He escaped and his people began to treasure the feathers and use them on their spiritual clothing.

Mainly girls perform the Sxwayxwey dance because two girls found the Sxwayxwey. Richard Malloway knew them. He claimed one was married in Sumas and the other was married at Musqueam. The latter's daughter went to live in Duncan; the former's daughter lived in Chilliwack. In this way the Sxwayxwey story has spread to Vancouver Island and Musqueam.

As a student member of the UBC Ethnographic Field School, Brian Thom conducted research into the life of Richard Malloway in March of 1993. He benefited from interviews that were recorded with Malloway by novelist and legal consultant Gordon Mohs.

MARY AUGUSTA TAPPAGE

In keeping with the British legal tradition of defining women as chattels of their husbands or fathers, the Indian Act of 1876 decreed that Aboriginal women who married non-Aboriginals could no longer be defined as Indians, and they automatically lost their band memberships. Their children were also deemed "non-status."

In essence, in order to be registered as an Indian in Canada, a person could either be defined as "a male person" or else "the wife or widow of a person who is entitled to be registered." This

BOOK JACKET PHOTO BY ROBERT KEZIERE

At age four, Mary Augusta Tappage was taken to a Catholic school in the Cariboo. "We were made to write on the board one hundred times, 'I will not speak Indian any more.'"

paternalistic system meant thousands of Aboriginal women, such as Mary Augusta Tappage, lost their Indian status as soon as they were married.

The Days of Augusta (1973) is a mixture of Tappage's prose and poetry, with evocative photos by Robert Keziere, which effectively tell her life story, as edited by Jean E. Speare. One of her stories was also posthumously edited for publication by Speare as *The Big Tree and the Little Tree* (1986).

Born in 1888 at Soda Creek in the Cariboo, Tappage was the daughter of a Shuswap chief and a Métis woman who had fled the prairies after the defeat of Louis Riel during the Riel Rebellion. She was sent to St. Joseph's Mission near Williams Lake where she was punished for speaking her Shuswap language. After nine years, she was permitted to live with her beloved grandmother. She was married, at age fifteen, to George Evans, the son of a

Welshman and a Shuswap mother of the Sugar Cane Reserve. Declared non-status, she retained her self-sufficient Aboriginal ways as they pre-empted 166 acres at Deep Creek.

The birth of her own first child influenced her choice of vocation as midwife. In *The Days of Augusta*, she recalls, "I was out feeding the cattle when I felt my first pain. Well, I kept on feeding the cattle, feeding the calves. . . . I was still sick. When that was over I came back to the house. I had to chop my own wood. Well, I finally fixed my bed and I was getting ready. I made a big fire and I opened the oven so it would be warm in the house.

"I kept getting worse and worse. Finally my daughter was born. All alone, I got up and fixed her up. . . . I had to clean myself up. . . . Made some more fire. Well, I was there for three days in bed and I got up. Well, in the meantime my husband came home. He had been on a spree for three days and came back drunk."

When her husband died, she decided not to re-marry. "Once is enough," she said. As described in her memoir, Tappage made her own clothes, shared her grandmother's stories, attended church, raised several homeless children and delivered babies. She taught herself midwifery from a book she bought in Regina at Eaton's for three dollars. "I learned it by heart," she wrote in a poem, "at night in my kitchen by candlelight."

Mary Augusta Tappage died on August 16, 1978, and was buried on the Soda Creek Reserve.

On International Women's Day, in March of 1984, federal Indian Affairs Minister John Munro announced Bill C-31 to allow Aboriginal women such as Tappage to regain their lost status. Not without its paternalistic trappings, this Bill would enable Indian bands, generally controlled by men, to determine which women could be reinstated. Bill C-31 received its royal assent on June 28, 1985, and directly affected some 16,000 Canadian Aboriginal women and their approximately fifty thousand children.

The first woman to be reinstated as an Indian in Canada was Mary Two-Axe Early on the Caughnawaga Reserve in Quebec. At age seventy-three, she had been leading the struggle for reinstatement for 20 years.

GLORIA CRANMER WEBSTER

In 1949 Gloria Cranmer was identified in the *Native Voice* newspaper as the "First Indian Girl to Study at UBC." She graduated in anthropology in 1956 and has since become an important linguist, filmmaker and author within the 'Namgis (formerly Nimpkish) First Nation of the Kwakwaka'wakw.

Born in Alert Bay on July 4, 1931, Gloria Cranmer Webster is a member of the influential Cranmer family that includes her brother Doug Cranmer, an artist. Their father Dan Cranmer and great-grandfather George Hunt both worked with Franz Boas who first came to Kwakwaka'wakw territory in 1886.

Gloria Cranmer as she appeared in a July 1949 newspaper story about her attendance at UBC

After the potlatch ceremonies were banned by the Canadian government in 1884, her father Dan Cranmer became famous for hosting one of the greatest potlatches in coastal history, on Village Island in December of 1921. After 17 years of preparation, the enormous gathering attracted white authorities under the direction of Indian Agent William Halliday who offered suspended sentences to 45 participants if they agreed to surrender ceremonial clothing and paraphernalia. Twenty men and women chose instead to go to Oakalla prison.

Confiscated materials from Dan Cranmer's potlatch were sent to Ottawa from Village Island, Alert Bay and Cape Mudge, and some were retained by Superintendent General of Indian Affairs

Duncan Campbell Scott for his private collection. Chief Mungo Martin eventually hosted the first legal twentieth-century potlatch in British Columbia in 1953, after the ban had been lifted in 1951.

After her graduation from UBC, Gloria Cranmer worked for two years as a counsellor for female prisoners who were first-time offenders at Oakalla Prison Farm. During her work for the John Howard Society she met and married John Webster, the executive director for the society in Saskatchewan, and their daughter was born in Regina. After 18 months in Saskatchewan, the family moved to the West Coast where Gloria Cranmer Webster worked as a counsellor at the YWCA in Vancouver, raised two sons, and became program director for the Vancouver Indian Centre.

In 1971, when Ottawa provided $2.5 million to build the UBC Anthropology Museum, she was hired at age forty to become an assistant curator at the new facility. While collating Northwest Coast artifacts for the museum, she became deeply involved in the successful repatriation of potlatch artifacts confiscated from her father's 1921 potlatch.

In 1975, the National Museum of Man in Ottawa agreed to return potlatch materials with the caveat that a museum had to be constructed to properly display and maintain the collection. Two museums were built, one at Cape Mudge, the other at Alert Bay where Webster served as Curator of the U'mista Cultural Centre (1980–1991). Potlatch artifacts have also been retrieved from the National Museum of the American Indian.

Able to speak and write Kwak'wala, Webster played a key role in the creation of the U'mista Cultural Centre, a facility modelled on a traditional Kwakwaka'wakw Big House. The Centre has since produced at least 12 Kwak'wala-language books for schools, and several award-winning documentary films including *Potlatch . . . A Strict Law Bids Us Dance* and *Box of Treasures*. Webster has also worked with Jay Powell to develop a spelling system to transcribe the sounds of the Kwak'wala language.

To document the Kwakwaka'wakw show that was presented by General Motors at Expo '86 in Vancouver, Webster supplied the text for *The Kwakwaka'wakw and the Spirit Lodge* (1986). The Spirit Lodge installation was so popular that it was recreated identically and installed at Knott's Berry Farm in Los Angeles.

In 1991, Webster curated the *Chiefly Feasts* exhibit at the American Museum of Natural History. She also contributed significantly to *Kwakwaka'wakw Settlement Sites, 1775–1920: A Geographical Analysis and Gazetteer* (1994) by Robert Galois.

Gloria Cranmer Webster received an honorary Doctor of Laws degree from the University of British Columbia in 1995.

DOREEN JENSEN

"The term 'Land Claims' is really a misnomer, we're not really claiming land because it's our land. I would just say that we are redefining our boundaries."—DOREEN JENSEN

Born in Kispiox in 1933, Doreen Jensen of the Fireweed clan was delivered by a medicine woman in her great-grandmother's bedroom. She commenced her work as an educator and carver in 1951.

A graduate of the Kitanmax School of Northwest Coast Indian Art in Hazelton, Jensen is fluent in Gitxsan and a founding member of the 'Ksan Association and the Society of Canadian Artists of Native Ancestry. "The Kitanmax School was started because we needed to reclaim our traditional performance arts for a play we were putting on called *Breath of Our Grandfathers*," she says. Work on the play began in 1953, but the Kitanmax School didn't open until after the 'Ksan Historic Indian Village was established in 1968. *Breath of Our Grandfathers* was performed in 1972 at the National Arts Centre in Ottawa.

Sister of Chief Walter Harris, Jensen curated the *Robes of Power* exhibit at UBC and co-wrote *Robes of Power: Totem Poles on Cloth*

VICKIE JENSEN PHOTO (NO RELATION)

My Great-Grandmother with Lip Labret *is a 1994 mask by Doreen Jensen, made of alderwood, horsetail, red-cedar bark, acrylic paint and abalone shell. In 1995, Jensen said, "We don't have a word in our language for 'art' because art was all around us."*

(1987). With Cheryl Brooks, she co-edited *In Celebration of Our Survival: The First Nations of British Columbia* (1991), a collection of writings and art for a special issue (#89) of *BC Studies.*

A 1995 interview with Doreen Jensen by Lynne Bell and Carol Williams appears in a double issue of *BC Studies* (#115–116) and Jensen is one of four Aboriginal artists featured in Loretta Todd's 1994 National Film Board documentary *Hands of History.* Her cousin Lonnie Hindle developed the phonetic system for the Gitxsan language with Bruce Rigsby, an American linguist.

HARRY ASSU

"There were so many fish in Discovery Passage then you could walk on them!"—HARRY ASSU

A professional fisherman for over half a century, Harry Assu traced his family and tribal history in *Assu of Cape Mudge* (1989), co-written with Joy Inglis and with illustrations by Hilary Stewart. It recalls his father's famous potlatch of 1911 and his first boat, a 12-foot cedar dugout fitted with oars. "I got paid fifty cents for each salmon at the cannery at Quathiaski Cove," Assu told Inglis.

Assu's father was renowned Lekwiltok chief Billy Assu (1867–1965) who brought the first gas boat to Cape Mudge, helped his sons outfit their first gill-netter, and convinced federal authorities to allow Aboriginals to become seine-boat skippers. The Assu family is well-regarded for guiding the Cape Mudge Band, the biggest of the four Lekwiltok bands in the Campbell River area, to prosperity and relative independence.

Harry Assu skippered his first seiner at age twenty-nine and bought his boat, the *BCP 45*, in 1941. Harry Assu took over the Cape Mudge chieftanship from his father in 1954. Five years later,

Harry Assu and Joy Inglis

when Assu was the oldest skipper in the B.C. Packers fleet, his seiner was selected to serve as the model for the engraving on the Canadian five-dollar bill. If you look carefully in the background of the "old" five-dollar bill, you'll also see a second seiner, *Bruce Luck*, which was owned by Assu's sons.

The Assu family is known for favouring entrepreneurial management of Aboriginal resources, having helped to form the Pacific Coast Native Fisherman's Association, forerunner of the Native Brotherhood.

"We were always able to take care of ourselves," Harry Assu told Inglis. "Indians don't join unions. I look at it this way. There is no help from the unions. . . . It's the company that gave you the job."

MARY JOHN

The indomitable Mary John, Sr., of the Stoney Creek Reserve was one of the founders of the Yinka Déné Language Institute and held the position of Permanent Honorary Chair. Tireless in her devotion to language preservation, she made by far the largest contribution to the Saik'uz Dictionary which now includes more than 8,000 entries. In 1980 she also co-founded the Stoney Creek Elders Society. A dignified survivor of racism and innumerable tragedies, she became Vanderhoof's Citizen of the

Year in 1979, the first Aboriginal to receive the honour.

Her memoir *Stoney Creek Woman: The Story of Mary John* (1989), co-written with Bridget Moran, chronicles the Carrier tribe from the arrival of missionaries and settlers in the Bulkley Valley to the present. Often reprinted, it received the Lieutenant-Governor's Medal for Historical Writing from the B.C. Historical Federation in 1990. For many years it was the bestselling title ever produced by Arsenal Pulp Press.

Born in Lheidli (Prince George) in 1913, Mary John was raised in Saik'uz. At the age of nine, she went to school in Fort St. James. She then moved to Lejac Residential School the next year when it was created. She left school when she was fourteen and married Lazare John when she was sixteen.

"Over the years, between 1930, when I was seventeen, and 1949, when I was thirty-six, I had 12 children, six girls and six boys. Some were born in the village, some on the trapline or at our hunt-

Mary John, 1988

ing grounds. Not one of my children was born in a hospital. My mother acted as a midwife for me; when I lost her, my aunts or other relatives were with me. Some of the midwives practised the old ways of Native medicine. We call it the laying on of hands. We believe that some Native women have a gift of healing in their hands. . . . And oh, that cup of tea that was brought to me after each child was born tasted so good!"

Mary John's story was recorded by social worker Bridget Moran who first visited Stoney Creek Indian Reservation in 1954. Born in 1923 in Northern Ireland, Moran made headlines in 1972 when she was evicted from the visitors' gallery in the Victoria legislature for staging an anti-poverty protest. Moran and Mary John met in 1976 at the time of an inquest into the death of another Stoney Creek woman, Coreen Thomas.

"I have vivid memories of Mary at that inquest," Moran recalled. "I remember watching her gather some of the young people together, speaking softly to them, advising them to tell the truth. . . . Time after time, as we talked together, I have heard her reconcile the irreconcilables, and laugh at the doing of it. I attended the Roman Catholic Church in Stoney Creek village with her, for example, and I heard that wonderful voice of hers soar over all the other parishioners as she sang, 'How Great Thou Art.'"

Mary John acknowledged the hardheartedness of the nuns and priests who controlled residential schools, and she believed the Canadian government and the church destroyed her people's language and culture, but she remained a devout Catholic until her death on September 30, 2004. She was known as Mary John, "Senior" to distinguish her from her daughter-in-law, Mary John, Jr.

HARRY ROBINSON

"I tell stories for 21 hours or more when I get started.
Kind of hard to believe, but I do, because this [is] my job.
I'm a storyteller."—HARRY ROBINSON

A longtime rancher and member of the Lower Similkameen Indian band, Harry Robinson was born in Oyama near Kelowna on October 8, 1900. He devoted much of the later part of his life to telling and retelling Okanagan stories that he first heard from his partially blind grandmother Louise Newhmkin on her Chopaka ranch.

Other mentors included Mary Narcisse, reputed to be one

ROBERT SEMENIUK PHOTO

Wendy Wickwire and Harry Robinson met in 1977 when he was living in Hedley.

hundred and sixteen years old when she died in 1944, John Ashnola, who died during the 1918-flu epidemic at age ninety-eight, as well as Alex Skeuce, old Pierre and old Christine.

"When I become to be six years old," he said, "they begin to tell me and they keep on telling me every once in a while, seems to be right along until 1918. I got enough people to tell me. That's why I know. The older I get, [it] seems to come back on me. . . . Maybe God thought I should get back and remember so I could tell. Could be. I don't know. I like to tell anyone, white people or Indian."

With the help of Margaret Holding, Harry Robinson learned to read and write English in his early twenties. Weary of itinerant ranching and farming jobs, Robinson bought his first suit from a second-hand store in Oroville and married Matilda, a widow about ten years older than him, on December 9, 1924. By the 1950s they had acquired four large ranches near Chopaka and Ashnola where Matilda had grown up as the daughter of John Shiweelkin.

Childless and burdened by a hip injury that occurred in 1956,

Harry Robinson sold his ranches in 1973, two years after Matilda died on March 26, 1971. On August 24, 1977, Robinson was living in retirement in a rented bungalow in Hedley when he met a non-Aboriginal graduate student from Nova Scotia, Wendy Wickwire, who was introduced by mutual friends. On the evening before they all went to the Omak rodeo in Washington State, Harry launched into a story after dinner and continued until almost midnight. That experience drew Wickwire back to the Similkameen Valley for the next ten years, with her Uher reel-to-reel tape recorder, transcribing and editing Robinson's stories, narrated by him in English.

For part of the 1970s, Wickwire lived in Merritt and Lytton, immersing herself in Aboriginal culture for a Ph.D. dissertation on Indian song. "I went to Lytton, to Spences Bridge, to Spuzzum, and all over to get a bigger cross-section of songs. Then I got to spend the whole year in the Nicola Valley, near Merritt, living in a cabin and tripping out to find people to record. During this time Harry kept telling me his stories."

Harry Robinson telling a story in 1985

Now a member of the Department of History and the School of Environmental Studies at the University of Victoria, Wickwire first broached the idea of putting Harry Robinson's stories into book form in 1984 and he approved. "I'm going to disappear," Robinson said, "and there'll be no more telling stories."

For years Harry Robinson would wait for Wickwire at the bus stop outside his home near Hedley, then invite her to climb into his old green Ford pickup truck so he could tell more stories. "We'd go out to dinner and he'd tell stories all night. The next day we'd drop around to all of the various places in town, buying groceries at the general store, or sightseeing or something, and I'd make him dinner, and then we'd spend another night telling stories. I'd come back and go to a rodeo with him, or go on a car trip, or something, and we'd always have a great time. Hanging out, we kind of became like a father and daughter."

This collaboration has produced three volumes of stories: *Write It On Your Heart: The Epic World of an Okanagan Storyteller* (1989), a finalist for the Roderick Haig-Brown Regional Prize when Robinson was eighty-nine; *Nature Power: In the Spirit of an Okanagan Storyteller* (1992), winner of the Roderick Haig-Brown Regional Prize in 1993; and *Living by Stories: A Journey of Landscape and Memory* (2005), containing Coyote stories and material about the new quasi-monsters, *SHAmas* (whites), who dispossess Aboriginals of their lands and rights.

"The third volumes contains many of the stories I put aside earlier because they were just too weird for words," says Wickwire. "For instance, Harry tells a story about a meeting between Coyote and the King of England. I saw nothing like them in the published collections.

"But after a detailed study, I have decided that Aboriginal folks a century ago were likely telling such far out stories—but the collectors weren't recording them very often. They weren't interested in them because they saw them as 'tarnished' stories. Franz Boas et al wanted the pure 'traditional' stories. Of course they were busy defining traditional in their terms, for their own purposes."

In his stories Robinson differentiated between stories that are *chap-TEEK-whl* and stories that are *shmee-MA-ee*. The former explain creation from a period when the Okanagan people were animal-people. The latter are stories from the world of human people, not animal people. He was always willing to incorporate modern influences, including the Judeo-Christian God, within his evolving world view.

"A good example of Harry's ability to incorporate current events in a meaningful way in his stories," writes Wickwire, "is his interpretation of the landing on the moon of the American astronaut Neil Armstrong. When the news of this event reached Harry, it was not surprising to him at all because he knew that Coyote's son had gone there years ago. The white people were naive, he concluded.

"Armstrong was not the first to land on the moon. He had simply followed the path that Coyote's son had learned about long ago, which is recorded in the old story 'Coyote Plays a Dirty Trick.' In this story, Harry sees the earth orbit and the moon orbit of the Apollo mission as the two 'stopping points' so critical to Coyote's son's return to earth."

Eventually Harry Robinson needed full-time medical attention for a worsening leg ulcer. He went to live at Pine Acres senior citizens home near Kelowna, in Westbank. "It was very sterile," Wickwire recalls. "He was used to driving his old pickup truck into town and getting his mail, and having lots of visitors come to his house." Robinson moved to a senior citizens home in Keremeos. Later his condition deteriorated when his artificial hip dislodged and caused serious infection. He had 24-hour care at Mountain View Manor in Keremeos until he died on January 25, 1990.

ANNHARTE

Born in 1942, Marie Annharte Baker is Anishinabe from the Little Saskatchewan First Nations in Manitoba. Raised as a neglected child in Winnipeg, a city she abhors for its racism, she was abandoned by her alcoholic mother when she was nine. After studying at universities in Brandon, Vancouver and Minneapolis (centre for the American Indian Movement), she

Annharte was touted as "the voice of today's urban Indian" in 1990.

left her husband and turned to social work and activism. Her poem "Me Tonto Along" from *Exercises in Lip Pointing* (2003) recalls the anguish and relief of her marriage break-up.

My old man was a good screw they say / all the ladies who changed his waylay / he took my money time any hour he pleased / cost me to see how his manhood freezed / kicked him out he kicked down the door / punched my face through the apartment floor / no way to stop him but once he caught zzz's / had my chance to plot his murder with ease / I pretend I let him move on to a next wife / Me Tonto along what I got left—my life

In one of 15 "five feminist minutes" commissioned by the National Film Board, Baker examined racial and sexual abuse of Aboriginal women. With her first collection of poetry, *Being on the Moon* (1990), Baker adopted the penname of Annharte as she reflected the voices and concerns of urban Aboriginal women. Her other books are *Coyote Columbus Café* (1994), *Blueberry Canoe* (2001) and *Exercises in Lip Pointing* (2003). Co-founder of the Regina Aboriginal Writers Group, Baker now lives much of the time on the West Coast.

GARRY GOTTFRIEDSON

A rancher and professional breeder of horses, Garry Gottfriedson is the son of Aboriginal parents who were both at the forefront of community activism in the era of George Manuel. "When you're born Indian," he says, "you are born into politics."

After living in the bush for eight years, Gottfriedson attended literary readings at the home of Jeannette Armstrong and at the En'owkin Centre in Penticton. After Armstrong submitted some

Garry Gottfriedson

of his poetry to a writing competition without his knowledge, he was awarded the Gerald Red Elk Creative Writing Scholarship by the Naropa Institute in Boulder, Colorado. Feeling estanged from his Shuswap roots, Gottfriedson studied writing under Allen Ginsberg, Anne Waldman and the pop singer/songwriter Marianne Faithful.

"I didn't even know who Allen Ginsberg was," Gottfriedson says. "When I got there I was shy. I was this bush Indian. I had hair down to my knees. I didn't speak to anyone outside my culture."

Gottfriedson has since gained his MFA in Creative Writing from the Naropa Institute and a Masters in Education from Simon Fraser University. Born and raised in Kamloops, he has taught at Cariboo College and served as a councillor and consultant for the Kamloops Indian Band.

Gottfriedson's historical work, *One Hundred Years of Contact* (1990), was followed by *In Honour of Our Grandmothers: Imprints of Cultural Survival* (1994), a collaborative coffee table book that included Cree artist George Littlechild and Reisa Smiley Schneider.

His poetry collection *Glass Tepee* (2002) contains cryptic and and lyrical perspectives based on his Secwepemc heritage:

Owl dance at Dukes / when the powwow season ends / wrapped in wannabe white girl clothes / labatts & between the sheets / they go all out / all the way / to the bee sting / arms slide around the shoulder/ of the smiling drunk / Mary Kay caked faces forget / that home is a mountain of people / sitting in bunch grass / puffing on Red Stone / sending pitiful words / into the air / hoping / for a Round Dance.

In addition, filmmaker Loretta Todd commissioned Gottfriedson to write "Forgotten Soldiers," a poem about Aboriginal war veterans in Canada, that served as the basis for a documentary. According to Gottfriedson, some returning Aboriginal veterans lost their treaty rights because a clause in the Indian Act prohibited them from taking up arms, for or against Canada.

He has also published a children's book, *Painted Pony* (2005), illustrated by William McAusland, in keeping with his work as a rancher. Along with his brother, who raises bucking horses for rodeos, Gottfriedson maintains the family tradition of breeding quarterhorses which he sells to buyers throughout North America. Fluently bilingual, he has developed his own teaching method for the Shuswap language, one that requires physical responses to learning individual words.

JOANNE ARNOTT

Now known sometimes by her married name, Joanne Arnott-Zenthoffer, Joanne Arnott was born in Winnipeg, Manitoba, in 1960. A Métis writer who facilitates Unlearning Racism workshops, she studied at the University of Windsor, then moved to British Columbia in 1982. Much of her writing concerns family relations, such as "Like an Indian: Struggling with Ogres," a pastiche of five prose poems to conclude *My Grass Cradle* (1992):

Joanne Arnott

My Family / some of us are sitting around the table, getting on for a change, peaceable, friendly. My sister, who always thought that my father was beautiful, tells him so. He hears it. She goes on, strokes his arm lightly and says, your skin is beautiful. Like an Indian. He jumps up, afternoon shattered by a girl's words saying the unsayable words, he storms from the room, a real electrical storm crackling and swirling through the rooms of our small house. Power of repression, power of lifetime and generations of denial, everything coming unhinged on an afternoon where he'd dared to relax for a moment with his children. Well you can't trust children. Never relax with them. They are crazy, and you never know what they might say . . .

I am not the only girl or woman of my generation / in my family learning to find safety in the truth. We struggle to unsilence ourselves, and to stop silencing each other: Not easy. We write letters, poetry, songs, and tell each other stories, from a distance, over time. Am I an Indian? Like an Indian? Or, as a dream-man told me with a loud guffaw, 'Better a little bit Indian than not Indian at all!' I am a woman who was a girl, Native and European, a parent who was a child who struggles with ogres. Now and then.

Arnott's first book of poetry, *Wiles of Girlhood* (1991), was written "for all the young women" and won the Gerald Lampert Award in 1992. Her other books include a children's book on natural childbirth, *Ma MacDonald* (1993), illustrated by Mary Anne Barkhouse; *Breasting the Waves: On Writing & Healing* (1995), a selection of candid personal essays on writing, healing and motherhood; and *Steepy Mountain Love Poetry* (2004).

As a mother to five sons and one daughter, Joanne Arnott-Zenthoffer lives in Richmond.

CONNIE FIFE

As a Cree mother and lesbian, Connie Fife viewed Canadians as living in "separate homelands" when she published *Poems for a New World* (2001).

Redolent with anger and sorrow, Fife's poems also extend an invitation for non-Aboriginals to sit "as equal partners at the banquet table of mother Earth."

Born in Saskatchewan in 1961, Fife graduated from the En'owkin International School of Writing in Penticton. Her poetry titles include *The Colour of Resistance* (1994), *Beneath the Naked Sun* (1992) and *Speaking Through Jagged Rock* (1999).

The Gustafsen Lake standoff. The Oka crisis. The shooting of Connie Jacobs when she refused to give up her children to Social Services. These were some of the subjects for the poetry of Connie Fife when she was living in Victoria.

Her poem "A Mother's Son" is dedicated to Jacobs and her nine-year-old son Ty who were shot to death on March 24, 1998, by an RCMP officer on the Tsuu T'ina Reserve in Alberta after Social Services attempted to apprehend Jacobs' three children. No charges were laid, giving rise to Fife's visceral and defiant poem of protest.

Connie Fife has recently moved from British Columbia to Winnipeg.

my son / I stopped the bullets / For as long as i could / until my heart was torn from my ribcage / and my shattered bone become flour on our kitchen flour / how I wept going down / down / to the moment when I could no longer withstand their bullets / your youth clearcutting a pathway / back into my arms when i held you up to the sun / singings praises for your birth

now i watch as righteous men / defend your murder / defend the onslaught of sliced corpuscle / and the tearing away of your muscle / and i sing / i sing your name into the mouth of every coming sunrise / and i will continue / until they know the significance of your birth / together with the act of stealing your life / and i will sing / and i will not stop

LOUISE FRAMST

Louise S. Framst of the Tahltan First Nation was born on May 29, 1944, in Lower Post, B.C., and raised in northern B.C. where she lives on a farm at Cecil Lake with her husband. With her B.Ed. (5-Year) in History and Special Education from UBC, Framst has experience as a teacher in a multi-grade rural school, a librarian and a learning assistant teacher.

Prior to her retirement, she served as an itinerant teacher facilitating programs for children with special needs. Framst has also edited a community project entitled *A Community Tells Its Story: Cecil Lake 1925–2000* (2000), and self-published three Tahltan cookbooks and a series of children's titles, including

Self-publisher Louise Framst

Manny's Many Questions (1992), *Kelly's Garden* (1992), *On My Walk* (2001), *But I Cleaned My Room Last Year!* (2002) and *Feathers* (2004).

"The reason that I chose to become my own publisher," she says, "is that it was important to me to have my own interpretation put on stories that I chose to publish. It seemed to me that if others edited my work, then somehow what was important to me might be 'lost' or misinterpreted."

LORNA WILLIAMS

Born in Mount Currie within the St'at'imx (Lillooet) First Nation, Lorna Williams trained at the B.C. Institute of Technology to become a nurse, but switched to education to specialize in First Nations instruction. In 1973, she became involved in the administration of the Mount Currie Community School, developing training for First Nations teachers to teach in their own language. Williams subsequently worked as the Native Indian Education Specialist with the Vancouver School Board and became involved in constitutional issues, both federally and in Europe, to ensure the representation of indigenous peoples. Lorna Williams received the Order of British Columbia in 1993.

Lorna Williams

Williams has served as director of the Cultural Centre and Curriculum Development for the Ts'zil Board of Education and she has created Lil'wat language curriculum materials such as *Exploring Mount Currie* (1982), adopted as a Grade Two text.

Illustrated by Plains Cree artist Mary Longman, Williams' second book *Sima 7: Come Join Me* (1991) describes the activities of a four-day youth gathering held on the banks of the Lillooet River. A Salteaux visual artist from the Gordon Band near Punnichy, Saskatchewan, Mary Longman Aski-Piyesiwiskwew is a Ph.D. candidate in Art Education at the University of Victoria who has also illustrated Beth and Stan Cuthand's bilingual children's book *The Little Duck/ Sikihpsis* (2003).

Mary Longman

ARDYTHE WILSON

The claim to ownership of approximately 22,000 square miles (or 58,000 square kilometres) in northwestern British Columbia by the Gitksan and Wet'suwet'en peoples first entered the courts in 1984 with the filing of the statement of claim. This high profile case was brought before B.C. Supreme Court Judge Allan MacEachern in 1987 and was heard over 374 days, ending in the spring of 1990.

Partially due to a ban imposed on courtroom photography, Don Monet of Hazelton attempted to capture the soul of the three-and-a-half-year-long sovereignty case with a collection of cartoons, portraits and sketches. These were combined with the notes and transcripts of Gitksan writer Skanu'u (Ardythe Wilson) for *Colonialism on Trial: Indigenous Land Rights and the Gitksan Wet'suwet'en Sovereignty Case* (1991).

Lawyers Stuart Rush and David Paterson at first argued unsuccessfully on behalf of Ken Muldoe (also known as Delgamuukw) and the Gitksan and Wet'suwet'en. Judge MacEachern ruled that Aboriginal rights in general exist at the "pleasure of the Crown" (accepting the Judgement in R. v. St. Catherine's Milling and

Colonialism On Trial *cover image*

Lumber Company [1885]) and are therefore extinguishable "whenever the intention of the Crown to do so is clear and plain."

MacEachern dismissed the evidence of academic experts who included Hugh Brody, Arthur Ray, Antonia Mills and Richard Daly. "The anthropologists add little to the important questions that must be decided in this case," he declared. MacEachern referred to Thomas Hobbes' *Leviathan* to characterize the lives of Gitksan and Wet'suwet'en ancestors as being essentially "nasty, brutish and short," and therefore too primitive to constitute an organized culture.

"The unique thing about about our nations is that we weren't nomadic nations," Ardythe Wilson says. "We were settled in ancient villages." Wilson's viewpoint has prevailed with the ratification of the Nisga'a Treaty in 2000, invalidating Judge MacEachern's earlier findings.

LIZETTE HALL

Containing reminiscences of the author's father Chief Louis-Billy Prince, grandson of Chief Kwah, *The Carrier, My People* (1992) by Nak'azdli elder Lizette Hall recalls Carrier culture and history specific to the Stuart Lake Carrier people.

"All the information in this book was given to me by my father who was past ninety-three years of age then," she writes, "who had an excellent memory and recalled everything with clarity. He gave me all the details in our Carrier tongue. If I don't make myself clear to the reader, please bear in mind that English is my second language."

Hall's material in-

Lizette Hall and her father

cludes the history of Chief Kwah and his missing dagger, the establishment of the Stuart Lake Mission by Fathers Lejac and Blanchet, memories of Father Nicholas Coccola, origins of the name Carrier, photos of Carrier WW II army veterans and descriptions of customs and beliefs. "The Carrier's method of showing contempt for another person is to approach the person with the back of the hand towards the victim's face. The back of the index finger is then rubbed quickly down the bridge of the victim's nose."

Louis-Billy Prince (1864–1962), son of Simeyon Prince, who was the son of Kwah, was a constable who accompanied the Oblate priest Father Adrien-Gabriel Morice as a cook on some of his explorations. After Father Morice arrived in British Columbia in 1880, he became the first person to make extensive and accurate recordings of any Athapaskan language in print. After Morice left Fort Saint James in 1904, he corresponded with Louis-Billy Prince for many years, asking questions about his language in order to compose *The Carrier Language,* published in 1932. Written in English and the Nak'azdli dialect of Carrier, *The Little Dwarves and the Creation of Nak'azdli* (1996) is a children's version of a legend told to Morice by Louis-Billy Prince.

DAVID NEEL

"Photographs are not objective. Once this is recognized, one can see a portrait for what it is: a result of an interaction between two people."—DAVID NEEL

A descendant of Kwakiutl carvers Ellen Neel and Mungo Martin, David Neel studied photography in the United States and returned to produce the text and photographs for *Our Chiefs and Elders: Words and Photographs of Native Leaders* (1992), followed by *The Great Canoes* (1995). His illustrations have also appeared

POSTCARD CIRCA 1950S

David Neel's uncle Mungo Martin created the world's tallest (and skinniest) totem pole. Erected in Victoria's Beacon Hill Park in 1956, the red cedar pole measures 127' 7".

in several other books, including Ellen White's *Kwulasulwut: Stories from the Coast Salish* (1981).

According to Elijah Harper in Neel's *Our Chiefs and Elders*, "public images of Aboriginal people have been almost completely negative," ever since the arrival of Columbus in 1492. Neel agrees with Harper. "For well over a hundred years, we have learned to accept a false image of the people of the First Nations," he says. "The tool used to build this image has been the camera."

Influenced by photographers such as Cartier-Bresson, Cornell Capa and W. Eugene Smith, David Neel was critical of the photos by pioneer photographer Edward S. Curtis whose massive series *The North American Indian* greatly influenced North American attitudes about Aboriginals. "When viewed as art," Neel concedes, "they are quite wonderful. However, they are very problematic when one starts to examine them for authenticity, integrity and general content."

Curtis frequently used wigs on his subjects and dressed his subjects in clothing that belonged to other tribal groups. "This visual cocktail is comparable to photographing a French woman in a traditional Italian dress and offering this as an image of an 'authentic' European," says Neel. Curtis' pan-Indian approach, born of a colonial mentality and feelings of white cultural superiority, has been endemic in Hollywood films. "When depicted in popular culture," says Neel, "we are either a 'noble savage' or a degraded heathen."

David Neel

Recognizing that we all live in a time of the created image and "if you do not create your own, someone will create it for you," Neel set out to photograph and interview elders, many of whom were the last witnesses to Aboriginal life before cars and gas-driven boats. In 60 duotone photos he provided dual depictions of his subjects, in both traditional dress and everyday dress. They included Harry Assu, Ruby Dunstan, Leonard George, Chief Joe Mathias, Bill Reid, Chief Saul Terry and Chief Bill Wilson.

"This body of work is intended to be the antithesis of the 'vanishing race' photographs of Native people," Neel wrote. "This is a statement of the surviving race."

David Neel was born in Vancouver in 1960 to Karen Clemenson, a non-Aboriginal, and David Neel, eldest son of Ellen Neel, one the few female carvers on the Northwest Coast. His Aboriginal name, Tla'lala'wis, meaning "a meeting of whales coming together," was inherited from his father, who received it from his uncle, Mungo Martin. Mainly raised in Alberta, David Neel returned to British Columbia and opened a commercial studio in Vancouver in 1987.

SHIRLEY STERLING

Shirley Sterling fictionalized her 1950s stint at the Kamloops Residential School in *My Name is Seepeetza* (1992), perhaps the first Canadian book for children about residential schools. The following year Sterling became the first Aboriginal author to win one of the province's top literary awards at the 1993 BC Book Prizes gala in Penticton.

The highlight of that evening was the presentation of the Sheila A. Egoff Children's Literature Prize to Sterling for her portrayal of the Niakapmux (Interior Salish) girl named Martha Stone, or Seepeetza, who struggles with the cruel contrast between her uncomfortable life at the Indian Residential School and her nourishing Aboriginal life with her brothers and sisters at Joyaska Ranch. Several members of Sterling's family from Merritt were in attendance at the ceremony.

"I genuinely didn't expect to win," Sterling told the audience.

"I have been writing since I was twelve years old and I thought perhaps when I retired at age sixty-five I would begin my writing seriously. But by an accident I ended up in Sue Ann Alderson's class in 1992. And if Sue Ann had not encouraged me I would never have written the book. And if my daughter Haika had not encouraged me I would never have sent it to the publisher. It was just the thrill of my life just to have been published."

During her acceptance speech, Sterling asked her mother to rise before the sold-out audience and acknowledge her integral role. "Mum, I want you to know that you've been the strength and the centre of our lives," Sterling said, "and you are the reason we've survived, and the reason that seven out of seven Native children went on to university to get a university education." Her mother also served as a role model for one of the main characters in Sterling's story.

Egoff Prize-winner Shirley Sterling, 1993

Sterling's story of Seepeetza closely mirrors her own experiences. Taken to a red brick building in Kamloops at age six, Seepeetza is forced to wear strange clothes, sleep in a dormitory with other Aboriginal girls, eat strange food and have her hair cut. The nuns call her Shirley instead of Seepeetza, or her nicknames Tootie or McSpoot. She is prohibited from talking "Indian," but her life is not entirely bleak. She enjoys the dance practices for school concerts and she takes comfort from her memories of home, always looking forward to summer vacations.

Born on the Joyaska Indian Reserve in 1948, Shirley Anne Sterling moved to Vancouver where she trained as a ballerina. She obtained her Ph.D. in Education and twice received the Native Indian Teacher Education Alumni Award, plus the Laura Steinman Award for Children's Literature. She died after a two-year battle with cancer on April 3, 2005, at Merritt, B.C.

CLAYTON MACK

Born in 1910 at Nieumiamus Creek, or "place of flies," Clayton Mack was a descendant of Bella Coola chiefs. He attended residential school and worked as a logger, fisherman and a rancher before becoming a tracker and hunting guide. A walking encyclopedia of tribal knowledge, he spent 53 years on the B.C. central coast, guiding the rich and famous on trophy hunts that felled an estimated 300 grizzly bears. In the 1960s he was flown to Hollywood where he reportedly mesmerized the California jet set with his hunting tales. His storytelling abilities led to his two collections of memoirs compiled and edited by his physician Harvey Thommasen, *Grizzlies & White Guys: The Stories of Clayton Mack* (1993) and *Bella Coola Man: More Stories of Clayton Mack* (1994).

Clayton Mack guided Thor Heyerdahl.

The story goes that when explorer Thor Heyerdahl was forced to remain in Canada in 1940, after Germany had invaded his Norwegian homeland, Heyerdahl befriended Mack who took him to see pictographs at Kwatna Inlet. Heyerdahl asked Mack if he thought it would be possible for his ancestors to have reached Hawaii in a dugout canoe and Clayton Mack suggested they might have used giant rafts of kelp. Later, Heyerdahl made his famous voyage in the South Pacific on a raft named *Kon-Tiki*. Clayton Mack suffered a stroke in 1988, moved into long-term care at the Bella Coola Hospital, and died in 1993.

HENRY W. TATE

Fluently bilingual, Henry W. Tate was a Tsimshian who taught at the Methodist mission school at Port Simpson. With the support of missionary Thomas Crosby, Tate first sailed aboard the mission boat *Glad Tidings* in 1894 with Captain William Oliver to spread Christianity as a lay preacher.

From 1903 to 1913, Tate forwarded his own versions of Tsimshian stories, written in English, to Franz Boas, who "cleaned-up" his informant's work and published it in 1916, with minimal credit to Tate, who died in 1914. When Simon Fraser University English professor Ralph Maud consulted the archives of Columbia University Library and saw the discrepancies between Tate's vibrant storytelling and Boas' revised texts for Boas' book *Tsimshian Mythology*, Maud blew the whistle on the famous anthropologist, first in an article for *American Ethnologist* called "The Henry Tate–Franz Boas Collaboration on Tsimshian Mythology." While criticizing the methodology that produced *Tsimshian Mythology*, Maud simultaneously resurrected the literary importance of Tate by arranging for publication of Tate's original versions of ten stories, as well as an extensive Raven cycle, in *The Porcupine Hunter and Other Stories: The Original Tsimshian Texts of Henry W. Tate* (1993). In this way Henry W. Tate's authority was acknowledged 79 years after his death.

Maud's opinionated analysis of Boas's relationship with Tate is recorded in *Transmission Difficulties: Franz Boas and Tsimshian Mythology* (2000).

ANNIE YORK

Born at Spuzzum in 1904, Annie Zechtgo York was an important Nlaka'pamux cultural authority, healer and oral teacher whose explanations of red ochre rock-writings found in the Stein Valley were published in *They Write Their Dreams on the Rock Forever* (1993), co-authored with Richard Daly and Chris Arnett.

With ethnologist Andrea Laforet of the Canadian Museum of Civilization, York also examined how the Nlaka'pamux people developed their separate sense of history, in comparison to non-Aboriginals, in *Spuzzum: Fraser Canyon Histories, 1808–1939* (1998).

As well, she provided information for books by the ethnobotanist Nancy J. Turner and Lytton Indian Band ethnobotanist Darwin Hanna.

One of seven brothers and sisters, York was educated in Pitt Meadows and moved to Merritt in 1925. A trained nurse, she served as an official translator in courts and hospitals for many years.

In 1932 she returned to Spuzzum where she later worked with Laurence and Terry Thompson to develop a dictionary of the Nlaka'pamux language. She died in 1991.

YALE MUSEUM & ARCHIVES #997.4.10.Q

Botanical expert and historian Annie York

SIMON BAKER

Raised primarily on the Capilano Reserve in North Vancouver, Simon Baker was the grandson of Joe Capilano. Born on January 15, 1910, he attended St. George's Residential School in Lytton. His life is recalled in *Khot La Cha: An Autobiography of Chief Simon Baker* (1994), written with Verna Kirkness. With an Aboriginal name meaning "Man with a Kind Heart," Baker served as a councillor to the Squamish Nation for more than 30 years, ten years as its chairman, and became the only Squamish member to be designated Chief for Lifetime.

Baker worked primarily as a longshoreman in Vancouver from 1935 to 1976, rising to the position of superintendent of Canadian Stevedoring. As a fundraiser and teacher, Baker played an important role in the First Nations House of Learning at the University of British Columbia where he received an Honorary Doctorate of Law in 1990. Ten years later he accepted the National Aboriginal Achievement Award for Heritage and Spirituality. Baker was invested in the Order of Canada in 1997.

In the periodical *First Nations Drum*, Baker was later referred to as "the last of the great North Shore Indians," a reference to a remarkable North Vancouver lacrosse team in the 1930s. Known as Cannonball Baker during his playing days, Baker was inducted into the B.C. Sports Hall of Fame in 1999.

Chief Simon "Cannonball" Baker

As a patriarch of nine children and 38 grandchildren, Simon Baker died on May 23, 2001.

GREGORY SCOFIELD

Born in Maple Ridge, B.C., into a Métis family of Cree, Scottish, English and French descent, Gregory Scofield never knew his father. "My parents were married in Whonnock, B.C. (a little town close to Maple Ridge), in 1964 under an alias name and spent the next two years in hiding, moving from province to province every couple of months," Scofield has recalled.

"Mom was surprised to find out that my father was already married and had a young daughter. In spite of this she stayed with him, and in 1965, while dodging the police in Port Alberni, B.C., she became pregnant with me. Not wanting to raise a baby on the run, she finally convinced him to turn himself over to the authorities. They returned to Maple Ridge where he turned himself in. Ironically, he ended up having a heart attack on the stand and beating most of the charges. I was born in July of 1966, the very day my father stood trial."

Scofield was separated from his mother at age five and sent to live with strangers. He grew up in northern Manitoba, northern Saskatchewan and the Yukon, struggling with substance abuse, poverty and racism. A sense of loss, poverty, alienation and self-hatred led to a profound sense of loneliness that he has traced back to his Red River settlement roots in a memoir called *Thunder Through My Veins* (1998) and

Gregory Scofield

Singing Home the Bones (2005), his new volume of poetry.

His first collection of poetry, *The Gathering* (1994), provides insights into Canada's Métis people and he received the Dorothy Livesay BC Book Prize. Scofield later received the Air Canada Award in 1996, which is given annually to a promising Canadian writer under age thirty. In *I Knew Two Métis Women* (1999) he recalls his mother Dorothy Scofield and his aunt Georgina Houle Young. He is also the author of *Native Canadiana: Songs from the Urban Rez* (1996) and *Love Medicine and One Song* (1997). Scofield has worked with street youth in Vancouver and been involved in the Louis Riel Métis Council. He currently lives in Calgary.

———❦———

GERRY WILLIAM

A member of the Spallumcheen Indian Band, just outside Vernon in Enderby, Gerry William of Merritt is Associate Dean at the Nicola Valley Institute of Technology. He has a B.A. in English Literature from the University of Victoria in 1985 and a Ph.D. in Interdisciplinary Studies. He first published a speculative fiction novel called *The Black Ship: Book One of Enid Blue Starbreaks* (1994), regarded as the first science fiction novel by a Canadian First Nations author.

Having taught at the En'owkin International School of Writing in Penticton, Williams, an avid "Trekkie" and sci-fi reader, believes science fiction contains themes and characters compatible with those used by Aboriginal writers.

In his follow-up novel, *The Woman*

Gerry William

140

in the Trees (2004), the character of Wolverine meets the young priest Black Robes in the Okanagan. This novel also features the character/spirit named Enid Blue Starbreaks, aka the Woman in the Trees, the woman from the other side of creation. The Woman in the Trees and Coyote observe and comment upon the "contact" period that brought disease and devastation to the Okanagan and Shuswap First Nations.

GERALD TAIAIAKE ALFRED

Holding a Canada research Chair at the University of Victoria, Gerald Taiaiake Alfred has been cited as one of the most influential figures in a new generation of First Nations leaders. He is one of the few Aboriginal authors who have heeded the admonitions of Howard Adams and undertaken scholarly, historical work. His history of Mohawk militancy and nationalism, *Heeding the Voices of Our Ancestors* (1995), was followed by an essay on ethics and leadership, *Peace, Power, Righteousness: An Indigenous Manifesto* (1999), and *Wasase: Indigenous Pathways of Action and Freedom* (2005).

Also known as Kanien'kehaka, Alfred was born at Tiohtie (Montreal) in the Kahnawake Mohawk territory where he has since served as an advisor on governance and land issues. After being schooled by Jesuits, Alfred had a stint as a machine-gunner in the U.S. Marine Corps.

He earned his doctorate from Cornell University and is known for his scholarly work on Native nationalism, Iroquois history and indigenous

Gerald Taiaiake Alfred

traditions of government. Born in 1965, Alfred resides in Songhees Nation Territory and works as Director of the Indigenous Governance Program at the University of Victoria. Taiaiake is a Mohawk name meaning "He's Crossed Over from the Other Side."

LEONARD GEORGE

Son of Chief Dan George, Leonard George is a North Vancouver psychologist and lecturer who has published two books pertaining to unorthodox beliefs and experiences.

Topics in *Alternative Realities: The Paranormal, the Mystic and the Transcendent in Human Experience* (1995) include Apparitions, Ghost Rockets, Burial Alive, Possession, Old Hag Experience, Incubus Nightmare, Devil's Jelly, Will-o'-the-Wisp, Zombification, Meditation, UFO abduction experiences and peyote.

Crimes of Perception: An Encyclopedia of Heresies and Heretics (1995) is "a compendium of those who held unorthodox views of reality, and, as often as not, ended up roasting on a stake or swinging from a rope." Topics include Gnosticism, Isochrists, Savonarola, Arius, Cathars, Free Spirits, Joan of Arc, Bruno, Rasputin, Paracelsus, Abulafia, Alistair Crowley, Mormons, Eckhart, the Great Witch Hunt, Alchemy, Kabbalah, Key of Solomon and Jesus Christ. George argues that heresy is necessary within society in order to provide provocative views of reality. "If one's certainties no longer work," he writes, "one may be forced to consider possibilities that one used to think were crazy."

Having succeeded his father as an elected chief of the Tsleil-Waututh First Nation in Burrard Inlet, George publicly confessed to severe problems with substance abuse and expressed a newfound determination to adopt a healthier lifestyle. Also a traditional singer and dancer, Leonard George served for seven years as executive director of the Vancouver Aboriginal Centre.

BARBARA HAGER

Optioned for a 13-part documentary television series on Aboriginal heroes, *Honour Song: A Tribute* (1996) by Barbara Hager profiles Susan Aglukark, architect Douglas Cardinal, athlete Angela Chalmers, Grand Chief Matthew Coon Come, artist Robert Davidson, health specialist Jean Cuthand Goodwill, actor Graham Greene, MP Elijah Harper, author Tom King, educator Verna Kirkness, hockey coach Ted Nolan, filmmaker Alanis Obomsawin, artist Jane Ash Poitras, Manitoba judge Murray Sinclair and pop singer Shania Twain. The book is used in First Nations schools and colleges to inspire young people.

Barbara Hager produces a syndicated current affairs television program from Victoria.

Barbara Hager was born in 1959 in Edmonton, the sixth of eight children, to a Cree/Métis father and a Scottish mother, George and Judy Todd. Her father died when she was twelve and the family moved to B.C. when she was fourteen. She completed high school in Hope, B.C., and studied English at Fraser Valley College. At seventeen she moved to Vancouver and took writing courses at UBC. In 1978 she was hired to write media releases and newsletters for the Department of Fish and Wildlife in Nanaimo. She wrote freelance articles on Vancouver Island, enrolled at Malaspina University-College, edited the student newspaper, and worked on the college's literary magazine.

After moving to Seattle and marrying musician Lee Hager, she ran a public relations company for the local music industry from 1980 to 1983, writing a Seattle music column for the *Georgia Straight* in Vancouver. She then moved with her (now former) husband to New York where she worked for one year at RCA Records and for five years at the city's Art Commission. She managed the Tweed Gallery for the city and wrote some culture-related speeches for Mayor Ed Koch.

Moving to Kentucky for three years, Hager published and edited a quarterly lifestyles magazine and founded the Central Kentucky Writer's Voice program at the Lexington YMCA. She returned to Canada and coordinated the 1993 and 1994 First Peoples Festival for the Victoria Native Friendship Centre. In 1994 she assisted in the delivery of the first National Aboriginal Achievement Awards which aired on CBC TV. This led her to write *Honour Song*.

For five years Hager worked as Aboriginal Liaison at the Royal British Columbia Museum. She then wrote her biography of Shania Twain, the country singer who was raised as an Ojibway. She conducted two interviews with Twain, one by phone and one in person, for a chapter in *Honour Song* called "Shania Twain: Buckskin and Cowboy Boots" and for her biography, *On Her Way: The Life and Music of Shania Twain* (1998).

In 2002, Hager was hired by CHUM Television to co-host *The New Canoe*, an Aboriginal arts and culture series on The New VI television station in Victoria. After the first season, CHUM sold the series to Hager. Since then she has produced the series independently through her company, Aarrow Productions. The fifth season of *The New Canoe,* airing in 2006, is co-hosted by Barbara Hager and Swil Kanim from the Lummi First Nation.

EDEN ROBINSON

B orn in 1968 on the Haisla Nation Kitamaat Reserve, Eden Robinson grew up near the mostly white community of Kitimat on the B.C. coast. Her uncle was author Gordon Robinson and her younger sister is CBC national news anchorwoman Carla Robinson.

Robinson first published *Traplines* (1996), a critically acclaimed collection of four short stories that she wrote in four months at UBC's Creative Writing department. Not necessarily autobiographical and mostly concerning dysfunctional families, *Traplines* won the Winifred Holtby Prize for best work of short fiction by a Commonwealth writer. It was also a *New York Times* Editor's Choice and Notable Book of the Year.

For many years Robinson struggled with *Monkey Beach* (2000), her first novel about a confused teenager coming to terms with her seventeen-year-old brother's disappearance at sea, probably by drowning. Subject to premonitions, the narrator, Lisamarie— named for Elvis Presley's daughter—explores Haisla community life on the central coast as the Hill family melds their Haisla heritage with Western ways. Lisamarie respects that her grandmother Ma-ma-oo is a guardian of tradition but she also has less tangible advisors—ghosts, sasquatches and animal spirits—as she journeys up Douglas Channel to Monkey Beach, a remote stretch of shore renowned for Sasquatch sightings.

There are forays up remote inlets, sasquatch sightings, bits of

Eden Robinson at BC BookWorld, 2000

Haisla vocabulary and a two-page explanation of oolichan grease, but at the heart of *Monkey Beach* is family intimacy. The novel received the Ethel Wilson Fiction Prize and was nominated for the Giller Prize. Her follow-up novel, *Blood Sports* (advertised for 2006), is set in Vancouver's Downtown Eastside.

RICHARD VAN CAMP

The Lesser Blessed (1996) is Richard Van Camp's coming-of-age novel about "skinny as spaghetti" Larry, a Dogrib teenager in the northern town of Fort Simmer. He sniffs gasoline, listens to Iron Maiden and copes with an abusive father, blackouts and an accident that killed several cousins.

"One time before the accident, I was hanging out with my cousins there. We used to play in the sand way down the beach. We'd take some toys down and build houses. We'd also sniff gas. I wasn't too crazy about it at first, but after seeing my dad do the bad thing to my aunt, it took the shakes away. I could feel the heat on my back from the sun. Every now and then we'd stop to eat or take a leak. Me and my cousin Franky were good pals, even though he was demented. He was the guy who told me that if you touch gasoline to a cat's asshole, the cat'd jump ten feet in to the air."

Larry befriends a newly arrived Métis named Johnny Beck and forges a more optimistic future. A German translation of *The Lesser Blessed* by Ulrich Plenzdorf, entitled *Die Ohne Segen Sind*, received the *Jugendliteraturpreis 2001* at the Frankfurt Book Fair in the juvenile category.

Born in Fort Smith, Northwest Territories, on September 8, 1971, Richard Van Camp is a member of the Dogrib (Tlicho) Nation from the Northwest Territories. Having gained his MFA from the University of British Columbia, Van Camp published a

Richard Van Camp

collection of short stories, *Angel Wing Splash Pattern* (2002), and two award-winning children's books, *A Man Called Raven* (1997) and *What's the Most Beautiful Thing You Know About Horses?* (1988), with Cree artist, George Littlechild. His collaboration with Littlechild was selected for an Our Choice designation from The Canadian Children's Book Centre.

Three of Van Camp's short stories have been turned into radio dramas with CBC and he co-wrote a screenplay for a short film, *The Promise*, for Neohaus Filmworks in the U.S.

Also a graduate of the En'owkin International School of Writing in Penticton and the University of Victoria's Creative Writing BFA Program, Van Camp wrote for CBC's *North of 60* television show for two months under their Writer Internship Program and was a script and cultural consultant for four seasons.

Published in numerous anthologies, Van Camp is a traditional and contemporary storyteller who teaches Creative Writing for Aboriginal Students at UBC and Aboriginal Media Art History at Imag(e).

In 1997 he received the Canadian Authors Association Air Canada Award for "Most Promising Canadian" under thirty. In 1999 he received the "Writer of the Year" Award for Children's Literature from the Wordcraft Circle of Native Writers and Storytellers for *A Man Called Raven*.

In 2002, Van Camp was honoured by the Northwest Territories' Living History Society for his career as a storyteller. In 2003, he was presented with the Queen Elizabeth Golden Jubilee Commemorative Medal.

MARION WRIGHT

Based on input from the elders of Quatsino, Fort Rupert and Gwa'sala-'Nakwaxda'xw, Marion Roze Wright gathered materials for an instructional guide to Kwakwaka'wakw culture entitled *My Elders Tell Me* (1996), rendered as a season-by-season story about two nine-year-old cousins who live near Port Hardy. Illustrated by Judy Hilgemann, this wide-ranging volume provides some Kwak'wala language terms and educational sidebars.

The Hamatsa Society, for instance, is introduced as comprising the high ranking members of society, usually young men who were sent into the forest to fend for themselves without hunting gear. The Hamatsa must encounter the cannibal man at the north end of the world, Baxwbakwalanuksiwe, who tries to control his

VICKIE JENSEN PHOTO

Contemporary Hamatsa ceremonial dancer at Alert Bay

149

human spirit. The Hamatsa then returns to his people who must catch and tame him, attempting to gain control of the supernatural cannibal spirit within him. At tribal gatherings the Hamatsa dances wildly to exhibit the spirit of Baxwbakwalanuksiwe but he is calmed by the sound of rattles. Similarly, Wright introduces the wild woman of the woods, Dzunuk'wa, as a child-stealing giantess who dances at the potlatch with a basket to gather children.

GREG YOUNG-ING

L ong associated with Theytus Books and the En'owkin Centre as an administrator and editor (as of 1990), Greg Young-Ing is a member of the Opsakwayak Cree Nation in Northern Manitoba. In his poetry collection *The Random Flow of Blood and Flowers* (1996), he writes about Métis status, racism, exploitation and colonialism.

Young-Ing has a Master of Arts degree in Northern and Native Studies from the Institute of Canadian Studies at Carleton University and a Masters of Publishing degree from the Canadian Centre for Studies in Writing & Publishing at Simon Fraser University. He has served as Chair of the Indigenous Peoples Caucus of Creator's Rights Alliance and variously contributed to The Royal Commission On Aboriginal Peoples, Assembly Of First Nations and Committee Of Inquiry Into Indian Education.

Young-Ing has also edited three volumes of *Gatherings,* once described as the only journal of literary writing by Aboriginal people in North America. *Gatherings – Volume III* (1992) explores *Mother Earth Per-*

Greg Young-Ing

spectives; Gatherings – Volume IX (1998) is subtitled *Beyond Victimization: Forging a Path of Celebration; Gatherings – Volume X* (1999) celebrates the publication's tenth anniversary. As well, he has co-edited *We get Our Living Like Milk From the Land* (1993–94) and *IndigeCrit: Aboriginal Perspectives on Aboriginal Literature* (2001).

In 2004, Anita Large replaced Greg Young-Ing as the publisher of Theytus Books. He is presently pursuing a Ph.D. in the Department of Educational Studies at UBC.

ROLAND CHRISJOHN

The findings from the First National Conference on Residential Schools held in Vancouver in June of 1991 were published in *The Circle Game* (2002), in which Roland Chrisjohn and his co-authors Sherri Young and Michael Mauran cited punishments used at the schools.

"Residential schools," according to Chrisjohn, an Oneida healer, "were one of many attempts at the genocide of the Aboriginal Peoples inhabiting the area now commonly called Canada. Initially, the goal of obliterating these peoples was connected with stealing what they owned (the land, the sky, the waters, and their lives, and all that these encompassed); and although this connection persists, present-day acts and policies of genocide are also connected with the hypocritical, legal and self-delusion needed on the part of the perpetrators to conceal what they did and what they continue to do."

The punishments of children cited in *The Circle Game* include sticking needles through the tongues of children and other areas of children's anatomy, often for prolonged periods; burning and scalding; beating to unconsciousness; breaking legs, arms, ribs, skulls and eardrums; using electric shock devices and forcing sick children to eat their vomit.

A list of more commonplace offences and punishments from an unnamed Oblate residential school has been provided in *You Are Asked to Witness* (1996), an excellent Stó:lo history edited by Keith Thor Carlson:

Communicating with girls: half hour of kneeling. Playing in school: kneeling down. Using tobacco: public reprimand. Late: confinement. Talking Indian: work during recess. Laziness: work during recess. Fighting: extra work. Talking in bed: extra work. Indian dancing: extra work. Playing forbidden games: extra work. Stealing apples: one day's confinement. Truancy: confinement and humiliation. Breaking plaster: three lashes. Disturbance in dormitory: a few slaps. Runaway: five strokes of the lash. Breaking into girl's dorm: expulsion. Setting fire to boys' dorm: expulsion.

A Haudenausaunee who received his Ph.D. in Personality and Measurement from the University of Western Ontario in 1981, Roland Chrisjohn has worked for 30 years in First Nations education, "suicidology" and family services. His co-authors Sherri Young and Michael Maraun are specialists in Applied Social Psychology and Statistics respectively.

ERNIE CREY

Ernie Crey and journalist Suzanne Fournier examined the devastating impact of large scale efforts to assimilate Aboriginals into mainstream Canadian society in *Stolen from our Embrace: The Abduction of First Nations Children and the Rebuilding of Aboriginal Communities* (1997), for which they received the Hubert Evans Non-Fiction Prize in 1998.

Crey was the executive director of the fisheries program for the Stó:lo Nation and a former president of the United Native

Suzanne Fournier and Ernie Crey

Nations. He had also worked as a social worker on behalf of aboriginal families. "As a child, I was forcibly removed from Stó:lo culture by social welfare authorities," he recalled. "Our family life was shattered after my eight siblings and I were split apart into separate foster homes. We were never again to reunite as a family. In so many ways, the history of my family is the history of aboriginal children in Canada."

MARILYN DUMONT

A s Harold Cardinal noted in a revised introduction to *The Unjust Society*, "The issue of 'Indian' and 'Métis' identity continues to be a contentious issue in Canada, particularly with regard to changes that have occurred since 1969 in the federal laws governing Indian status and in the self-description employed by the Indian First Nations and the Métis. The Métis, having secured

PHOTO BY BARRY PETERSON & BLAISE ENRIGHT-PETERSON

Métis poet Marilyn Dumont at the Havana Restaurant, Vancouver, 1998

express constitutional changes, have yet to sort out many issues related to how their citizens are to be recognized by the governments of the country." Recognition for Métis within the Aboriginal movement throughout Canada can also prove problematic.

In support of Louis Riel, militarist Gabriel Dumont led the Métis during the North-West Rebellion of 1885.

Born in 1955, as a descendant of the Red River freedom fighter Gabriel Dumont, Marilyn Dumont is a writer of Cree/Métis ancestry who has continued the struggle to assert the legitimacy of Métis identity.

In her prose poem "Leather and Naughahyde," Dumont has evoked the frictions that can sometimes ensue between "Indians" and "Métis" on a private level:

> So, I'm having coffee with this treaty guy from up north and we're laughing at how crazy "the mooniyaw" are in the city and the conversation comes around to where I'm from, as it does in underground languages, in the oblique way it does to find out someone's status without actually asking, and knowing this, I say I'm Metis like it's an apology and he says, "mmh," like he forgives me, like he's got a big heart and mine's pumping diluted blood and his voice has sounded well-fed up till this point, but now it goes thin like he's across the room taking another look and when he returns he's got "this look," that says he's leather and I'm naughahyde.

Marilyn Dumont has taught Creative Writing at Simon Fraser University and Kwantlen College, and worked in video production. She received the Gerald Lampert Memorial Award for *A Really Good Brown Girl* (1997) and her second collection of poetry, *Green Girl Dreams Mountains* (2001), received the Stephan G. Stephansson Award for Poetry from the Writers Guild of Alberta in 2002.

MARY LAWRENCE

Born to a single mother in Tonasket, Washington, Mary Lawrence was raised on the Vernon Indian Reserve where her grandmother was a full-blooded Okanagan. After a stint in residential school, she and her siblings were placed in a series of dysfunctional foster homes.

Lawrence studied writing at the En'owkin Centre and first published *In Spirit & Song* (1992). Her autobiography *My People, Myself* (1997) recalls how she overcame residential school, addictions, spousal abuse and incarceration in a California correctional facility. "For the troubled young woman who drifted into places that left her depressed and suicidal," Lawrence wrote, "I honour her."

Lawrence concludes by recalling her visit to the site of the Cranbrook Indian Residential School with her best friend Marge. "Thoughts and emotions flooded my body as I approached the large door. Then I felt the strongest emotion of all – RAGE! I visualized Sister Lois standing over me with her fat tummy bulging underneath her black habit as she held the strap with her right hand. I could see her round, fat face puffing up and getting ready to swing the strap upon me. I wanted to stomp on her shiny black shoes and run and hide."

The memoir was partially inspired by Beatrice Culleton's *In Search of April Raintree*, Shirley Sterling's *My Name is Seepeetza* and Celia Haig Brown's study of the Kamloops Residential School, *Resistance and Renewal.*

Mary Lawrence with her
baby Michelle

In 1997 Lawrence was pleased to report she had been able to "abstain from getting involved in addictive relationships with the opposite sex" for the past ten years. As of 2004, Mary Lawrence was living in Westbank, B.C., having raised her two daughters.

HEATHER SIMENEY MACLEOD

A member of the Métis Nation Northwest Territories, Heather Simeney MacLeod is a poet and playwright who came to live in the Thompson-Nicola Valley during the writing and publication of *The Burden of Snow* (2004). Having spent some of her teenage years in Carcross, she has recalled her northern past in a prose poem:

> *I know how to use an ulu; I've seen an Inukshuk in the midnight sun on the Barrenlands. Ask me anything. I have eaten whitefish, pike and char; I've served muskox burgers at the Wildcat Café. I worked the dishpit before the dishwasher went in and wore raingear and rubber boots and watched through the flapping of the screen door as Dave wind-surfed over Back Bay. I fed Tracy's dog, Bug, scraps from plates, drank coffee with Baileys through my shift and went back in the middle of the night, after the bars closed, for wine, beer, a snack. Ask me anything. I swam nude in Long and Great Slave lakes; had picnics in the cemetery. Ask me anything. I remember The Rec Hall, the worn path between it and The Range; I remember Saturday afternoon jams with Mark Bogan singing Wild Thing (Wild meat, you make a great treat; muskox, I gotta get lots).*

The Burden of Snow is a poetry collection in which she traces "bloodlines, trap lines and ancestral migrations" from Ireland, Scotland and Russia to the British Columbia interior.

"I used to live in the Arctic," MacLeod writes, "a place where

Heather Simeney MacLeod

my Indian blood found room to live, elliptical it moved within me, solid as snow." While living in Victoria, MacLeod published a collection of poetry, *My Flesh the Sound of Rain* (1998).

Her other books include *Shapes of Orion* (2000) and *The North Woods* (2003).

VERA MANUEL

Vera Manuel is a healing workshop coordinator who has also been the manager of Storyteller Theatre in Vancouver. As a playwright Manuel has dramatised accounts of abuse and helplessness in *Two Plays About Residential School* (1998), a dual publication containing stageplays by herself and Larry Loyie. Her *Strength of Indian Women* is about four elders preparing for a teenage girl's coming-of-age feast. In the process, they share secrets of their incarceration in residential schools.

"I didn't make up the stories told in *Strength of Indian Women*," she says. "They came from pictures my mother painted for me with her words, words that helped me see her as a little girl for the first time. Each time we staged a performance of the play, I mourned that little girl who never had a childhood. I mourned the mother missing from my childhood, and I gave thanks for the mother who became my loving teacher in adulthood, who had the courage to say the words I'd longed to hear, 'I'm sorry I wasn't there to protect you when you were a little girl.' Other stories came from feelings attached to the little knowledge I held of my father's experience as residential school and tuberculosis sanitorium survivor, a world of violence and isolation."

BARRY PETERSON PHOTO

Vera Manuel is the eldest daughter of George Manuel and Marceline Manuel.

For the twentieth anniversary celebration of the Union of B.C. Indian Chiefs (UBCIC) held in Kamloops in 1989, Vera Manuel prepared a brief history of the UBCIC, an organization that was created in reaction to the White Paper Policy of the federal government "that was intended to do away with Federal responsibility for Indians, transferring jurisdiction for Indians and Indian lands over to the provincial government."

Vera Manuel's 18-page history records that the UBCIC was formed in Kamloops after 150 delegates from throughout British Columbia convened at the residential school facility. That formative meeting was chaired by Chief Dennis Alphonse of the Cowichan Nation and Chief Clarence Jules of Kamloops. The first official headquarters for the UBCIC was on the Musqueam Reserve. Vera Manuel's father joined the UBCIC for two terms as its president after he had resigned from the National Indian Brotherhood.

WILLIAM BEYNON

William Beynon's name was first recorded in ethnographic literature in January of 1915 when Marius Barbeau wrote, "I am very fortunate in having gotten the services of Wm. Beynon, a very intelligent young half-breed Tsimshian, who proves more useful still in working directly with informants for me. He records myths quite successfully and with good speed."

It would take another 85 years before Beynon's writing would appear in book form, fully credited, despite his prolific career sending field notes to Barbeau in Ottawa. The notebooks of William Beynon are often considered among the most significant written records of Northwest Coast potlatching. They were published for the first time in *Potlatch at Gitsegukla: William Beynon's 1945 Field Notebooks* (2000), edited by Margaret Seguin Anderson and Marjorie Halpin.

Born in 1888 in Victoria to a Welsh father and Tsimshian mother, William Beynon had an extensive career as an ethnographer of Tsimshian, Nisga'a and Gitksan communities. His grandfather on his mother's side was Clah (aka Arthur Wellington) who taught the missionary William Duncan how to speak Tsimshian in 1857 and who has been credited with saving Duncan's life when he was held at gunpoint by the highest ranking chief of the Tsimshian.

Schooled in Victoria, William Beynon was the only one of six brothers who learned to speak Tsimshian from his mother. He did not finish the equivalent of high school. After working for the Canadian Pacific Railway and the Department of Public Works, he went to Port Simpson for the funeral of his uncle, Albert Wellington, in 1913, and decided to stay among his mother's people.

In the 1920s, Beynon began sending his field notes to Barbeau in Ottawa. Considered the founder of folklore studies in Canada, Charles Marius Barbeau was a native of the Beauce region south of Quebec City who first came to British Columbia in 1914. He later played a significant role in the "discovery" of Emily Carr by the fine arts establishment in Ontario. Although Barbeau incorrectly theorized that totem poles were only erected after contact with Europeans, he was one of the first ethnographers to attempt to document the accomplishments of individual Haida artists.

By 1948, Barbeau was paying Beynon $35 per notebook. Beynon otherwise supported himself by working in the fishing and canning industries of the north Pacific coast. In 1945 Beynon observed, and par-

William Beynon

ticipated in, two weeks of masked dramatizations and potlatching at the Gitksan village of Gitsegukla, where the focus of the ceremonies was the raising of five totem poles, four by Houses of the Gisgahest (Fireweed) crest group and one by a House of the Laxsel (Frog) crest group.

By the time he died in 1958, Beynon had sent approximately 54 notebooks to Ontario between 1929 and 1956. The notebooks from 1945 were later edited by Margaret Seguin Anderson and Marjorie Halpin. In reference to the gathering at Gitsegukla they wrote, "We are left with a deep appreciation not only for the immense amount of work done by Beynon, but also for the profound debt owed to the elders of Gitsegukla, who saw so clearly that their ways are the continuing strength of their people and who, in 1945, brought the young people of their village from reluctant acquiescence in these events to a deeper awareness and celebration of their identity and heritage."

PETER JOHN

"The best ship you can jump on is friendship."—PETER JOHN

Born on July 20, 1925, in the Carrier village of Sheraton on Burns Lake, located about 25 kilometres east of the town of Burns Lake, Peter John told the story of his life to Burns Lake Secondary School teacher-counsellor Doris Johnson for *Highu Yalht'uk / Elders Speak: The Story of Peter John* (2000), developed with the assistance of the Burns Lake Band.

The son of a trapper and muleskinner, he was taken to Lejac School east of Fraser Lake in 1935 to learn English. At age twelve, he had to rise every morning at 4 a.m. to milk cows for 45 minutes. "I soon learned there was a benefit to it. Whenever I was hungry, I could drink fresh milk, straight from the cow. I would

Peter John overcame demon alcohol to become a valuable community teacher.

fill my mouth about a dozen times before my stomach was filled. I never let one cow get away from me without feeding me. I was the healthiest kid in the school! They didn't know why, and I didn't tell them."

He worked briefly for the CNR before working at sawmills throughout northern B.C. for most of his life. He retired to Burns Lake where he became involved in the B.C. Association of Non-Status Indians (BCANSI) and the Burns Lake Native Development Corporation with George Brown. In the 1970s they persuaded Babine Lake Forest Products to build a sawmill at Sheraton and employ more than 100 Aboriginal workers.

In the late 1970s Peter John changed his life by successfully renouncing alcohol and cigarettes. "I asked God to help me," he said. "If I hadn't quit smoking and drinking, I'm sure about it: I wouldn't be here today. I'd be living on the streets in Prince George or Vancouver or somewhere. I'd be looking in dumpsters for things I could sell to get booze, to get drunk. Believe me, many people that I loved in this life are gone because of cigarettes and alcohol." To preserve his Aboriginal language, Peter John became increasingly active in the Yinka Déné Language Institute.

LEN MARCHAND

Leonard Stephen Marchand became the first Aboriginal from British Columbia to be elected to Parliament in 1968 when he defeated Davie Fulton and became a Liberal MP for Kamloops-Cariboo. (Louis Riel, a Métis, was elected to the federal parliament in 1873 and 1874 but was not allowed to take his seat.)

Marchand became secretary to Jean Chrétien when he was Minister of Indian Affairs and also became the first Aboriginal to serve in the federal cabinet when he was named Minister for Small

Business by Prime Minister Trudeau in 1976. The following year he became Minister of Environment and remained in that post until his defeat in the 1979 federal election.

After a stint as head of the Nicola Valley Indian Administration, Marchand became an honorary chief of the Okanagan Nation and a member of the federal Senate in 1984, remaining in office until his retirement in 1997.

Born in Vernon on November 16, 1933, in a family with eight children, Marchand lived on the reserve until age twenty-three. He graduated from the University of British Columbia in 1959 and the University of Idaho in 1964, having completed a Master's thesis on B.C. sagebrush. During the 1960s he was employed at the Range Research Station at Kamloops and at the Agricultural Research Station in Smithers.

His co-written memoir entitled *Breaking Trail* (2000) appeared the year after he received the Order of Canada. Although hardly a Red Power advocate, Marchand, a *Skilwh* or Okanagan Indian, agreed the term Indian was absurd. "If it were up to me, I'd be called a Déné. . . ." he wrote. "It's a dignified sounding name; it's easy to say; a lot of Canadians already recognize it; and it just means 'people' or 'person,' depending on how many you're talking about. Maybe a generation or two from now, we Indians will have found a name for ourselves that we can feel good about."

Len Marchand

165

BARRY PETERSON PHOTO

Marie Clements

MARIE CLEMENTS

In 2004, Marie Clements received the Canada-Japan Literary Award for her play *Burning Vision* (2003), which was also nominated for six Jessie Richardson Theatre Awards. *Burning Vision* is an impressionistic drama about Aboriginal miners in the Northwest Territories who were told they were digging for a substance to cure cancer, but instead were helping to build the atomic bombs that devastated Hiroshima and Nagasaki.

In 1930, Gilbert and Charles LaBine staked a claim for high-grade pitchblende near Cameron Bay on Great Bear Lake, in the Northwest Territories. When this Eldorado claim began extraction procedures, Déné men were hired to transport the ore and ferry it to Fort McMurray. In 1941, the U.S. government ordered eight tons of uranium from Eldorado for military research purposes. In 1942, the year the Canadian government bought control of the mine, the U.S. government ordered 60 tons of Port Radium ore. The first atomic bomb was exploded in New Mexico on July 16, 1945. Atomic bombs were dropped on Hiroshima on August 6, 1945, and on Nagasaki on August 9, 1945.

In 1960, the first Déné miner died of cancer in connection with the Eldorado minesite. As *Burning Vision* reveals, it was not until 1999 that the federal government signed a commitment to clean up and contain the Port Radium mine site, although a Canadian government publication had issued warnings about the health hazards of high-grade radioactive ores in 1931. Clements shows how race played a role in the miners' deaths.

Marie Clements was born in 1962. She founded Urban Ink Productions, a Vancouver-based Aboriginal and multi-cultural production company that creates and produces Aboriginal works of theatre, music, film and video. As a Métis performer and playwright, she has explored the politics of race, gender and class in *Age of Iron,* produced at the Firehall Arts Centre in Vancouver and published within *DraMétis: Three Métis Plays* (2001).

Clements' surrealistic play *The Unnatural and Accidental Women* (2005) is another politicized reconstruction of the past, this time pertaining to a 30-year-old murder case involving female victims of violence on Vancouver's Skid Row. After several women are found dead, all with high blood-alcohol readings, and all last seen with Gilbert Paul Jordan, a low-lifer known for his associations with primarily middle-aged Aboriginal women, a coroner lists these deaths as "unnatural and accidental."

GHANDL
(WALTER MCGREGOR)

In the fall of 1900, young linguist John Swanton (1873–1958) took the steamer *Princess Louise* north from Victoria towards Haida Gwaii and received his first Haida lessons on board from master carver Daxhiigang, known in English as Charlie Edenshaw (1839–1920). Swanton's way was charted by his mentor, anthropologist Franz Boas, who understood the need to document Haida culture in an era when the overall Haida population was estimated to consist of perhaps only one thousand people.

John Swanton arrived in Haida country from Harvard when the Haida were being ravaged by European diseases and assimilated by the missionaries. More than 90 percent of Haida villages were abandoned. When Swanton found approximately 700 Haida in the mission villages of Skidegate and Masset, he hired a teacher, guide and assistant named Henry Moody to help him accurately record Haida stories and oral history from an hereditary chief named Sghiidagits. Swanton paid his co-worker Moody $1.50 per day, six full days a week.

Swanton also paid poets, singers and storytellers 20 cents an hour and budgeted $35 per month, a princely sum at the time, for this purpose. "If we compare these rates to Swanton's own workload and salary," writes editor Robert Bringhurst, "we will find that he was paying his Haida colleagues pretty much the same hourly rate he was making himself."

During the year that followed, Swanton transcribed the oral work of Haida poets, most notably Skaay or Skaii (John Sky) and Ghandl (Walter McGregor), the so-called "Homer" of Haida literature, who was born around 1851 on the northwest coast of Moresby Island. The other three main storytellers were Kingagwaaw, Haayas and Kilxhawgins.

Bringhurst's first critical explorations of Swanton's work in his effort to revive the stories of Skaay, Ghandl and their Haida contemporaries was *A Story as Sharp as a Knife: The Classical Haida Mythtellers and Their World* (1999).

He then went on to compile a series of stories in *Nine Visits to the Mythworld: Ghandl of the Qayahl Llaanas* (2001). This volume features stories told by Ghandl, a Haida man in his fifties, blinded by either smallpox or measles. The name Ghandl means creek or fresh water. A missionary christened him Walter McGregor.

Swanton and Ghandl spent approximately a month painstakingly dictating and recording poetry. "Why Ghandl of the Qayahl Llaana of Qaysun has not also been adopted with full honours into the polylingual canon of North American literary history I do not know," writes Bringhurst. "He seems to me a great deal more accomplished—and therefore far more worthy of celebration as a literary ancestor—than any Canadian poet or novelist who was writing in English or French during his time."

Ghandl's style was rhetorical and unfettered by overt cleverness, as evidenced by the outset of "The Way the Weather Chose to Be Born," the opening selection in *Nine Visits to the Mythworld*. Bringhurst's version begins:

There was a child of good family, they say, / at Swiftcurrent Creek. / And her father had one of his slaves / constantly watching her. / She said to the slave, / "Tell that one I want to make love to him." / The day after that, / when she was out of doors with the slave, / she asked if he'd said / what she told him to say.

And the slave said to the young woman, / "He says he's afraid of your father." / But the slave had spoken to no one. / The slave was in love with her, they say. / When she had decided on somebody else, / she gave the slave the same instructions. / He failed again to deliver the message. / He told her again / that the man was afraid of her father.

After sending the message to each of her father's ten nephews, / the one of good family made love with the slave, they say. / And her father found out what had happened. / So they all moved away from her, they say. / And no one but her youngest uncle's wife / left food for her, they say.

She went digging for shellfish, they say. / After a while, she dug up a cockleshell. / The cry of a child came from inside it....

SKAAY (JOHN SKY)

The third volume of Robert Bringhurst's homage to Haida storytellers and tribal historians is *Being in Being: The Collected Works of a Master Haida Mythteller SKAAY of the Qquuna Qiighawaay* (2001), again based on the original ethnographic work by linguist John Swanton.

Born in the village of Qquuna around 1827, Skaay devoted his life to telling stories after he was crippled by an injury in middle age. Also known as John Sky, he lived most of his adult years in the village of Ttanuu. Both SKAAY and the other formidable Haida storyteller Ghandl belonged to the Eagle side of the Haida, as opposed to the Raven side.

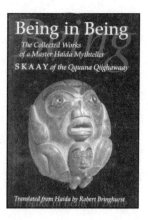

With a Haida intermediary who spoke English, Skaay dictated the story of his maternal lineage to Swanton at Skidegate in October of 1900, as well as the most extensive version of the Raven story ever recorded on the Northwest Coast. Swanton also transcribed what Bringhurst calls "the largest and most complex literary work in any Native Canadian language," an epic poem called *The Qquuna Cycle*, with 5,500 lines. It begins:

> *There was one of good family, they say. / She was a woman, they say. / They wove the down of blue falcons / into her dancing blanket, they say. / Her father loved her, they say.*
>
> *She had two brothers: / one who was grown / and one who was younger than she. / And they came to dance at her father's town, they say, / in ten canoes, / and they danced, they say, / and then they sat waiting, they tell me.*
>
> *And someone—her father's head servant, they say— / went out and asked them, / "Why are these canoes here?"*
>
> *"These canoes are here for the headman's daughter." / The headman answered them, they tell me: / "Better look for other water." / They left in tears they say.*
>
> *They came to dance again on the following day, / in ten canoes, they say, / and again they were questioned, they say. / "Why are these canoes here?"*
>
> *"These canoes are here for the headman's daughter." / And then he refused them again, / and they went away weeping. . . .*

According to Bringhurst, who estimates Skaay's work amounts to 15 percent of Swanton's Haida opus, Europeans had been visiting Haida Gwaii for more than a century prior to Swanton's visit, but he was the first outsider to request stories told in Haida. "No outsider asked again for seven decades after that," Bringhurst claims, "and by then there was no one alive who had actually known the pre-colonial Haida world."

Among Swanton's Pacific Northwest publications are *Haida Texts and Myths, Skidegate Dialect* (1905), *Contributions to the Ethnology of the Haida* (1905), *Haida Texts–Masset Dialect* (1908), *Social Conditions, Beliefs, and Linguistic Relationship of the Tlingit Indians* (1908), *Tlingit Myths and Texts* (1909), *Haida Songs* (1912) and *The Indian Tribes of North America* (1952). His unpublished southern Haida manuscripts were brought to the American Philosophical Society Library in Philadelphia in 1942. A 1940 festschrift to honour his career excludes mention of his early work in B.C.

LARRY LOYIE

"Don't let anyone steal a good story you remember. Write it down. The written word strengthens our oral tradition."—LARRY LOYIE

Larry Loyie was born in Slave Lake, Alberta, where he spent his early years living a traditional Cree life. At the age of ten he was placed in St. Bernard's Mission residential school in Grouard, Alberta.

"We had no more family life," he recalled, "and we weren't allowed to speak our language. Mostly what I learned there was how to pray and how to work and how to sing Latin at Mass. We got to go home once every school year, though many children stayed the whole year. It was basically worse than jail. Everything that was natural to a small child was a sin and we got punished for it.

"I didn't know about sin and heaven and hell until I got there,

The writing projects of Constance Brissenden and Larry Loyie include AIDS education.

and then I was always getting beatings from the nuns. I ran away twice and both times I was caught and severely beaten. After that I started reading everything I could get hold of. There were classics like *Huckleberry Finn* but there was exactly nothing about Native people. We were punished for the fact that hundreds of years earlier Jesuits had been killed by Native people. I lost all feeling about my Native heritage."

At fourteen, Loyie left school to work on farms and in logging camps. At eighteen, he joined the Canadian Forces, living in Europe before returning to work in northern British Columbia and Alberta. "Through it all," he says, "the longing for the traditional First Nations way of life I experienced as a child always stayed with me."

Many years later, in Vancouver, he went to the Carnegie Centre at Main and Hastings to upgrade his education and writing skills, and to learn typing. In 1991, he travelled around British Columbia to interview Native teachers for two radio documentaries. The following year he co-edited an anthology for novice writers called *The Wind Cannot Read* (1992), having travelled across Canada to collect material for a 1,000-page manuscript.

One of his writing instructors, Constance Brissenden, quickly realized she was learning as much from him as he was learning from her. Their partnership and mutual concerns led to the creation of a new writers group called Living Traditions, in which Loyie blossomed as an educator and as an author of several plays, short stories and a children's story dealing with residential schools, native traditions and literacy.

Loyie's first play called *Ora Pro Nobis (Pray for Us)* (1998) was based on his residential school years. It was first staged in Vancouver and five federal B.C. prisons in 1994, then at the Weesageechak Festival in Toronto in 1995. Excerpts from the play are included in *Away from Home: American Indian Boarding School Experiences, 1979–2000* (Heard Museum, 2000).

Loyie wrote two more plays: *Fifty Years Credit*, based on the media's view of First Nations people, performed at Carnegie Community Centre in 1998; and *No Way to Say Goodbye*, a commission for the Aboriginal AIDS Conference in northern Alberta in 1999. All of his plays have benefited from his association with Brissenden.

For Loyie's autobiographical children's book, *As Long as the Rivers Flow* (2003), Loyie and Brissenden toured Canada to present more than 90 readings. As a result of Loyie's voice ailment, Brissenden reads the text; Loyie responds to questions. This poignant memoir recalls Loyie's last summer of freedom before he was forced to attend residential school.

It was Cree artist George Littlechild who suggested Loyie write the story for children. "I told George about the truck that picked us up and took us away," Loyie says. "The sides were so high, we could only see the sky."

Illustrated by First Nations artist Heather Holmlund, *As Long as the Rivers Flow* reflects Loyie's perspective at age nine as he cares for an abandoned owl, watches his grandmother make moccasins, helps the family prepare for a hunting trip and receives a new name, Oskiniko—meaning Young Man—a name he still uses. Children are fascinated by the story of Larry's tiny grandmother, Bella Twin, who reputedly shot the biggest grizzly bear in North America. First Nations communities are using the book in classrooms, at conferences, and for healing purposes. Some listeners are moved to tears.

In mid-September of 2003, Loyie was singled out for an honour dance at the Niagara Native Friendship Centre in St. Catherine's where more than two hundred people lined up to shake hands with the writers, then gathered behind them as they danced slowly around the arbour while drummers sang a special song. "Being recognized by my own people this way," says Loyie, "was the greatest honour I could have."

Loyie received a 2001 Canada Post Literacy Award for Individual Achievement and the 2003 Norma Fleck Award for *As Long as the Rivers Flow*. His essay on First Nations people of the Lower Mainland appears in *The Greater Vancouver Book*, edited by Chuck Davis. Brissenden and Loyie have also co-written an AIDS educational story, *The Gathering Tree* (2005), illustrated by Heather Holmlund, in which a 21-year-old athlete returns for an Aboriginal gathering and educates his young cousin about his illness.

EARL MAQUINNA GEORGE

Chief Earl Maquinna George entered the University of Victoria at the age of sixty-four and earned a B.A. in History and an M.A. in Geography. His memoir *Living On The Edge: Nuu-chah-nulth History from an Ahousaht Chief's Perspective* (2003) was written from his Master's thesis to inform his children, grandchildren and all the people of Ahousaht about their past.

In *Living on the Edge*, he provides a detailed account of the whale hunt, beginning with the carving of the giant whaling canoe (over 40 feet long and six feet wide) from a special cedar log that has its own history. He also gives a step-by-step description of the ritual killing of the whale, and ends with the dividing up and sharing of the meat afterwards.

The section "The Gift of Salmon" records the special care taken in ensuring the continuing fertility of the salmon stock. The book concludes with Maquinna's thoughts about the ongoing treaty process. Since many issues in the treaty process relate to ownership, he explains the word *HaHuulhi*: "It is not ownership in the white sense; it is a river or other place that is shared by all Nuu-chah-nulth-people, with a caretaker being hereditary chief of each site or village." It is now a concept recognized in the negotiations, and has been written into the framework as one of the key issues.

Maquinna was taught Christianity during his early years at a United Church residential school where he remained fulltime because his mother died when he was young and his father worked as a fisherman. His education at school was complemented by traditional training from the elders of the Ahousaht First Nation, of which he is an hereditary chief. He also learned fishing and sea-going skills, worked with the Coast Guard, and earned his skipper's papers. A stint as a logger gave him first-hand knowledge of the damage caused by logging companies.

Earl Maquinna George

Gloria Nahanee (second from right, back row) and family

GLORIA NAHANEE

When Gloria Nahanee attended St. Paul's Indian Day School in the 1950s, she was taught Scottish, Irish, Ukrainian, Dutch, Spanish and square dances by nuns, but there was no Aboriginal dancing at the school. When the Squamish Nation held their powwows in the 1940s and 1950s, lasting up to ten days, she sometimes ran away and hid at the other end of the field.

"I thought I had to dance," she recalls in *Spirit of Powwow* (2003). "The regalia and the noise scared me at first. But I can remember the stage where our ancestors Uncle Domanic Charlie and

August Jack did the Squamish songs and dances."

Powwows at Squamish disappeared for 30 years after 1958. It was not until Nahanee's own daughter began spontaneously to dance at age six that she began to explore the traditional dances of her own culture. Nahanee travelled to powwows for two years and co-founded the Squamish Nation Dancers in 1987, then organized a revival of the Squamish powwow in 1988.

"The old spirits told me they wanted the powwow revived," she says, "and that our young people would carry this on." The annual Squamish powwow is now a three-day event that attracts some two hundred dancers and an audience of up to four thousand. *Spirit of Powwow* is Nahanee's introduction to, and celebration of, powwow dances and traditions, co-written with Kay Johnston.

PHILIP KEVIN PAUL

The son of Aboriginal rights activist Chief Philip Paul, co-founder of the Union of B.C. Indian Chiefs and the National Native Brotherhood, Philip Kevin Paul grew up on the Saanich Peninsula where he still lives.

Paul received a B.A. from the University of Victoria. Prior to the publication of *Taking the Names Down from the Hill* (2003), winner of the Dorothy Livesay Prize for best book of poetry by a B.C. author, his writing appeared in various anthologies. Much of it concerns death and family relations, such as his short poem "Patient."

I heal my mother / by sitting in this room / with her.
I heal her / in the prayer / of three slow cups of tea.
In the hospital / for two months, / she wants just / small details
/ about our house.
We close our eyes / and see each room / one by one.

Paul accepted his Livesay Prize on May 1, 2004, at Victoria's Government House with a speech in English and his traditional language Sencoten. He described his debut collection as an elegy to Saanich and to his parents, while thanking his adopted "poetry parents" Patrick Lane and Lorna Crozier.

Kevin Philip Paul

As an amateur lightweight boxer, he was once ranked fifth in B.C. and 13th in Canada. Paul has worked as an instructor at the Saanich Adult Education Centre and he lives on his Aboriginal homeland in Brentwood Bay.

MARIA BOLANZ

As a mother and daughter team, Maria Bolanz and Gloria C. Williams have examined the significance of Tlingit carvings of interior house posts, portal entrances and free standing totem poles with their crests in *Tlingit Art: Totem Poles & Art of the Alaskan Indians* (2003). Although the Tlingit are primarily residents of Alaska, the Taku Tlingit (Inland Tlingit) are based in Atlin, B.C.

Maria Bolanz is a descendant of the Blackfoot Nation and, through marriage to a Tlingit, she became a member of the Carcross/Tagish First Nation in Canada and a member of Cook Inlet Regional Corporation in Alaska. She received a B.A. from Western College in Oxford, Ohio, and an MA from Stanford University. After retirement, she secured a degree in

Maria Bolanz

anthropology from the University of Alaska.

Her daughter Gloria Williams is a member of the Taku River Tlingit First Nation in Canada, the Tlingit/Haida Tribe in southeast Alaska and the Cook Inlet Regional Corporation (a corporation that was formed in relation to the Indian land claims settlements made in Alaska). After studying at the University of Alaska, she has worked at the Alaska Native Medical Center in Anchorage.

AGNES ALFRED

The first autobiographical portrayal of a Kwakwaka'wakw matriarch, *Paddling to Where I Stand, Agnes Alfred, Qwiqwasutinuxw Noblewoman* (2004), recalls the life and times of Agnes Alfred (1890?–1992), a storyteller of the Kwakwaka'wakw First Nation who was jailed for her participation in a potlatch in 1922. It was translated and transcribed by her granddaughter, Daisy Sewid-Smith, along with Martine J. Reid.

Her extraordinary lifespan and her status as a Qwiqwasutinuxw noblewoman meant she had access to a vast store of traditional knowledge, especially in her role as a mediator between the natural-human-profane realm and the supernatural-sacred realm. Agnes Alfred did not speak English and she had no Western education, but she had skills in remembering and storytelling, as well as memorizing myths, chants and historical accounts.

The birth of Agnes Alfred was recorded on a rock on Village Island. She converted to Christianity as a child, but later took upon herself the task of passing her traditional knowledge to younger generations. In a chapter entitled "Myth Time," for instance, she tells the story of the girl who was dragged into the underworld to live among the Halibut people. Years later this girl reaches for one of her father's halibut hooks, and so returns to her parents.

After French-born Martine Reid came to UBC as a Ph.D. student in 1975, she began to participate in a program to preserve the heritage of Aboriginal peoples—and that led her to "Mrs. Alfred." When Reid met Agnes Alfred, she was a widow of about eighty, but still independent and living alone in the big house built by her husband for her and their thirteen children in Alert Bay. It was her habit during the fall and winter to make a cycle of pilgrimages to visit her many relatives and descendants in Campbell River and elsewhere.

Reid would accompany Agnes Alfred on her annual visits, and thus she met Daisy Sewid-Smith, a Kwak'wala language instructor at the University of Victoria. The three women eventually formed a partnership—with Mrs. Alfred dictating her memoirs, Daisy Sewid-Smith acting as translator, and Martine Reid transcribing and editing.

Agnes Alfred's voice—by turns authoritative, humorous, poetic, and gnomic—rings out clearly.

"Poor me; I was married at such a young age. . . . They sailed away with me right away, and they brought me to this logging camp. . . . I had not even menstruated yet. I was perhaps only twelve or thirteen. I was really young. I was married for quite some time before I menstruated."

The chapter entitled "Becoming a Woman" describes the onset of menstruation and an elaborate ritual that marked Alfred's passage into womanhood. She was secluded from the rest of her household for twelve days, concealed by a curtain in a corner of a room. During this time, she sat (wearing the hat reserved for nobility), and was cared for by her mother and the tribal elders.

Agnes Alfred

E. RICHARD ATLEO

E. Richard Atleo, whose Nuu-chah-nulth name is Umeek, is a hereditary chief who teaches in the First Nations Studies Department at Malaspina University College. He has served as co-chair of the Scientific Panel for Sustainable Forest Practices in Clayoquot Sound. In *Tsawalk: A Nuu-chah-nulth Worldview* (2004), he introduces an ontology drawn from Nuu-chah-nulth origin stories. Tsawalk basically means "one" and it encapsulates an understanding of the universe as an integrated and orderly whole, expressed as "heshook-ish tsawalk"—everything is one.

E. Richaed Atleo, Ahousat, mid-1970s

Chapters include Tsawalk: Origin Tales and the Nature of Reality & How Son of Raven Captured the Day; Utl-cla He-xwa: The Struggle for Balance; Xaata-tsa Thluch-ha: Getting Married; Muu Quis-hai-cheelth: One Who Transforms; Suh-tcha Thlawk-thlawk-qua: A Humble Petition; Nuu-Pooh Tloo-utl-ish-sum: Remember Me; Utl-Pooh Heshook-ish Tsawalk: Everything Is One.

CHRIS BOSE

A member of the N'laka'pamux Nation, formerly known as the Thompson people of the Spuzzum area, Chris Bose is a musician and artist who was born in Merritt, B.C., on March 27, 1970. Bose is a self-described very tattooed ex-vegetarian who does not drink alcohol, smoke or do drugs. For awhile, he quit drinking coffee when a friend told him Aboriginal people around the world are being displaced from their lands by coffee growers.

Chris Bose

He has been a cobbler, a radio DJ, a bookstore clerk, president of the student body at the local University College, a farm labourer, and homeless. He has lived in Stockholm, Sweden, and Austin, Texas. His creative non-fiction narrative, also described as a novel, is *Somewhere in this Inferno* (2004). It reflects the struggles of a young man who is troubled by existential questions and cultural adaptation. Bose's writing has appeared in numerous anthologies, he has released several CDs of his music, and he is currently "surviving on grants, goodwill and urban hunting and gathering."

<hr />

HAROLD EUSTACHE

A Shuswap member of the North Thompson Indian Band, Harold Eustache revisited a traditional story for his first novel *Shuswap Journey* (2004) about the abduction of Shuswap women by a tribe from over the Rocky Mountains during the period of early colonization. A chief's daughter relates her predicament as her father looks for her in the Rockies. The idea for the story was passed along from Eustache's great-great aunt. Augusta Tappage confirmed such abductions occurred in her memoir *The Days of Augusta* (1973).

Harold Eustache

JOSEPH O'CONNOR

Joseph O'Connor (b. 1948), Natasha Netschay Davies (b. 1971) and Lloyd Dolha (b. 1960) co-edited an anthology of *First Nations Drum* newspaper articles entitled *Smoke Signals from the Heart* (2004).

For the 800,000 Aboriginal people in Canada, *First Nations Drum* has been a vital link. During its 14 years as a national newspaper, *First Nations Drum* has run many profiles on Aboriginal role models such as Buffy Sainte-Marie, actor Adam Beach, hockey player Jordin Tootoo, artists Bill Reid and Robert Davidson, and guitarist-songwriter Robbie Robertson. A cover story in 2000 featured the missing women of Downtown Eastside—many of whom are Aboriginal—as a follow-up to the *Drum*'s 1997 coverage of the issue. Another cover design featured Premier Gordon Campbell with a Hitler moustache and Gestapo outfit, clutching *Mein Referendum,* in reference to the controversial public vote in response to Aboriginal land claims in B.C.

Smoke Signals from the Heart also recalls the confrontations at

Oka, Ipperwash and Gustafsen Lake, the 1997 Delgamuukw decision, elders, wild horses, Mohawk Ironworkers, the Lubicon Cree's boycott of the Calgary Olympics, powwows, Aboriginal gangs and the KKK in the Prairies. B.C. women profiled include Kootenay Chief Sophie Pierre, dancer and model Theresa Ducharme, filmmaker Barb Cranmer and psychotherapist Margaret Vickers— who hosted the first art exhibit by her brother Roy Henry Vickers.

M. JANE SMITH

A member of the Wolf Clan from the House of Wii Kaax, M. Jane Smith is a traditional Gitxsan storyteller and Simalgax language teacher who learned her narrative skills as a child while spending summers in a fish camp on the Skeena River. During the day, her grandmother would tell her stories about the trickster Raven and the Naxnok bird; in the evenings, when her uncles and grandfather returned home, she would hear more stories. "That is when the confidence was instilled in me," she says.

Although Smith was initially uncomfortable with the responsibility of recording oral histories, elders encouraged her, explaining the need for the stories to be preserved and treasured like a chief's regalia. "When you tell a story you credit your sources," says Smith, "and the listeners realize they are hearing a story that goes all the way into the beginning of time." *Returning the Feathers: Five Gitxsan Stories* (2004), reflects her respect for her elders, with the title referring to lost feathers from a chief's headdress.

M. Jane Smith

"I used to have a scientific mind," Smith says, "and thought [the stories] could never have happened . . . but when I took them and believed them and applied them to my life, I knew I was a storyteller. I come from storytellers and I want it said of me, she told a good story."

Returning the Feathers is illustrated by Gitxsan artist Ken Mowatt, an instructor of silkscreening and carving at the 'Ksan School in Hazelton. He was also raised in Gitanmaaxs and is a member of the House of Djokaslec.

LOUISE BARBETTI

A "rememberer" among the Haisla, Louise Barbetti has worked with many linguists and anthropologists over the decades. In that process she has co-authored, edited and contributed to *We are our History – A Celebration of our Haisla Heritage* (2005).

In the preface to her dictated version of the "Haisla Nuyem," the tribal traditional law, Barbetti writes, "My name is Amais Adec'. That's my feast name. My retirement name is Ajigis. I was born on this reserve almost 70 years ago. This was a time when the Haisla people, young and old, were still governed by the *nuyem*, our law. I grew up listening to my great grandmother and, later, my mother teaching us the *nuyem* through the old stories. *Nusi antlanuxw waxganutlanuxw,* they told us the stories every night. Our *nuyem* is still important. Our young people need to learn our law, our *nuyem*. That's the reason I'm putting it down. The *nuyem* will keep us as strong and capable as our ancestors were."

Born in 1936 at Kitamaat Village, *mujilh* (chieftainess) Louise Barbetti, sister of chief C'esi, has also been a leader in the movement to preserve the Kitlope region.

JAY POWELL PHOTO

Louise Barbetti

TOMSON HIGHWAY

Commissioned by Western Canada Theatre and the Secwepemc Cultural Education Society, Tomson Highway's play *Ernestine Shuswap Gets Her Trout* (2005) is set in British Columbia during the visit of Prime Minister Sir Wilfrid Laurier to the Thompson River Valley in August of 1910. The central characters are four women, representing the four seasons, preparing a feast for Laurier's visit. Tomson Highway is not generally associated with B.C., but he came to Kamloops to help produce the cabaret style play that premiered with an Aboriginal cast in 2004. It was the subject of an hour-long Bravo! television documentary in 2004: *Tomson Highway Gets His Trout*, from Getaway Films, directed by Tom Shandel, who has described Highway's work as being "at once light-hearted burlesque and angry agitprop."

Ernestine Shuswap Gets Her Trout was produced to mark the importance of a treatise written in 1910 by James Teit, on behalf of 14 chiefs of the Thompson River basin, to assert their collective rights to land and resources.

Written in the spirit of Shuswap, a "Trickster language," *Ernestine Shuswap Gets Her Trout* was mounted in the style of Highway's preceding play *Rose* (2004), the third instalment of his "rez" cycle set on the Wasaychigan Hill Reserve, the same venue for *The Rez Sisters* (1986) and its sequel *Dry Lips Oughta Move to Kapuskasing* (1989). His production notes for *Rose* advise, "Think of the exercise as just a bunch of kids, the kind you were when you were five years old, playing in and with a chest filled with old clothes and objects. . . .

"And last, the old—and very tiresome—question: 'should only native actors have the right to play native roles?' (Which to me has always sounded a lot like: 'should only Italian actors have the

MURRAY MITCHELL PHOTO

Janet Michael and Lisa Dahling await Prime Minister Laurier in the Belfry Theatre production of Ernestine Shuswap Gets Her Trout, *by Tomson Highway, 2005.*

right to play Italian roles?' Or: 'Thought Police productions presents an all-German-cast in *Mother Courage* by Bertolt Brecht. Only Germans need apply.')"

To make clear his feelings on the issue of "Aborginals Only" theatre, Highway has pleaded "in my Cree heart of hearts" for an end to political correctness, if, for no other reason, than it will enable him to have his plays produced more often.

The eleventh of twelve children, Tomson Highway was born in a tent near Maria Lake, near Brochet, Manitoba, in 1951. After six years in his nomadic Cree family, he attended a residential school in The Pas where his introduction to music escalated into ambitions to become a concert pianist. He composed music for Aboriginal theatres and festivals, joined the Native Earth Performing Arts Company in Toronto in 1984, and worked with his brother René, a dancer and choreographer. Both brothers were openly gay. Tomson Highway's only novel, *Kiss of the Fur Queen* (1998), is based on events that led to his brother René's death of AIDS.

Twice a recipient of the Dora Mavor Moore Award, Highway is Canada's best-known Aboriginal playwright and the first Aboriginal writer to receive the Order of Canada.

In 1910, Chief Louis Xlexlexken of Kamloops addressed Prime Minister Wilfrid Laurier, reciting a speech written by James Teit. Here are some of his words:

"We welcome you here, and we are glad we have met you in our country. We want you to be interested in us, and to understand more fully the conditions under which we live. When the *seme7uw'i*, the Whites, first came among us there were only Indians here. They found the people of each tribe supreme in their own territory, and having tribal boundaries known and recognized by all. The country of each tribe was just the same as a very large farm or ranch (belonging to all the people of the tribe). . . .

"They [government officials sent by James Douglas] said that a very large reservation would be staked off for us [southern Interior tribes] and the tribal lands outside this reservation the government would buy from us for white settlement. They let us think this would be done soon, and meanwhile, until this reserve was set apart, and our lands settled for, they assured us that we would have perfect freedom of travelling and camping and the same liberties as from time immemorial to hunt, fish and gather our food supplies wherever we desired; also that all trails, land, water, timber, etc., would be as free of access to us as formerly.

"Our Chiefs were agreeable to these propositions, so we waited for treaties to be made, and everything settled."

James Teit (centre, back row) accompanied [back row] Chiefs Eli Larou (Shuswap), John Tetlenista (Thompson), Thomas Adolph (Lillooet), William Pascal (Lillooet) and [front row] Chiefs James Raitasket (Lillooet), Johnny Chilitsa (Okanagan), Paul David (Kootenai) and Basil David (Shuswap) to Ottawa in 1916.

Ellen Neel with her "Totemland" tourist design, 1950

III
ARTISTS &
CARVERS

FRANCIS BATISTE

Born on the Inkameep Reserve near Oliver on December 6, 1920, Francis Batiste received the name Sis-Hu-Lk, meaning "always moving, always on the go," from his grandfather, Chief Batiste George. Encouraged by art teacher Anthony Walsh, who arrived to teach at the Inkameep Day School in 1932, Batiste was selected to illustrate the publication of a Native nativity tale with his pen and ink drawings in 1934, when he was fourteen. Two years later his drawings received commendations when they were exhibited in a children's display of the Royal Drawing Society in London, England. In 1940, Batiste was awarded the Bishop Johnson Gold Medal by the Catholic Women's League for his contribution to Canadian culture. With the help of his grandfather, Batiste studied art in Santa Fe, New Mexico, for a year and continued to exhibit his art, signing the name Sis-Hu-Lk.

In 1941, the Group of Seven artist Lawren Harris sponsored Batiste's attendance at a conference of Canadian Artists in Ontario, but Batiste stopped painting a year later with Anthony Walsh's departure to serve in World War II. In 1942, two thousand copies of the *The Tale of the Nativity*, written by Walsh and the children of Inkameep, with illustrations by Batiste, were published by the Committee to Promote the Revival and Development of the Latent Gifts of the Native Tribes of B.C., as engineered by Alice Ravenhill. This book imagines the birth of Jesus, as if it had occurred in the Okanagan Valley instead of Bethlehem.

In 1944, the CBC broadcast a version of the *The Tale of the Nativity* on Christmas Day. In 1951, some of Batiste's paintings were acquired by the B.C. Provincial Archives. At the instigation of his son, Chief Sam Batiste, the Osoyoos Indian Band has since reprinted the *The Tale of the Nativity*.

Charlie George illustration Klaquaek Kidnapped by the Whale *for* Soogwilis *(1951)*

CHARLIE GEORGE

Although the medical doctor Richard Geddes Large is credited as the sole author of *Soogwilis* (1951)—a Kwakiutl epic about a hero who encounters supernatural creatures, marries Klaquaek and confronts his human nemesis, Pahquees, an old medicine man—it was primarily the work of Charlie George of Fort Rupert, an outstanding carver and artist.

According to Large, his father (Dr. R. W. Large) received the 33 colour drawings within *Soogwilis* from Charlie George in the early 1900s when George was a young patient at the Bella Bella Hospital. Large, Jr., incorrectly described some of the illustrations as being "undoubtedly crude" and explained how he came by the text that accompanies the paintings. "Many years later it was my good fortune to meet the artist and hear from his lips the stories which were meant to go with the pictures. The drawings have undoubted value as ethnological data. Most of the text is the original story [of Soogwilis, the central character] as told by Charlie George, but I have included two additional tales gathered in later years from other Indians, but all of Kwakiutl origin."

Thanking folklorist Marius Barbeau for "his helpful criticism," Large, Jr., proceeded to blend the stories of Charlie George into one narrative in his attempt to "make this book at once ethnologically correct and interesting to the reader." Charlie George has never been recognized as one of the first Aboriginal authors of the province.

HENRY SPECK

One of the earliest attempts to seriously discuss and promote Kwakiutl art in print for commercial purposes was Henry Speck's 16-page catalogue *Kwakiutl Art* (Vancouver: Indian Designs Ltd., 1963) published by New Design Gallery to accompany Speck's first exhibition of 40 watercolours, from March 25 to April 4, 1964. It contained Speck's depictions of supernatural beings from Kwakiutl mythology—including tsonoqua, sea monster, raven, crane, sea wolf, beaver, halibut, sea raven, grizzly bear, frog, killer whale, owl, wolf, otter, octopus, sea eagle, king-of-the-sea and sisiutl—with an essay ("Kwakiutl Art: Its Background and Traditions") by Audrey Hawthorn, curator of the UBC Museum of Anthropology. It was re-issued in book format in 1964 and sold for $1.50. All the artwork was available to consumers in silk screen prints, 19" by 24.5". Having once earned one dollar per letter while painting names onto fishing boats, Chief Henry Speck became artistic director of Chief James Sewid's Kwagiutl Big House project that was completed at Alert Bay in 1965.

Born on August 12, 1908, on Turnour Island (also known as

Kalugwis), Speck attended the Alert Bay residential school for two years and was initiated as a Hamatsa dancer within the Tlowitsis tribe at age fourteen during a potlatch hosted by his uncle, Chief Bob Harris. As a member of the Pentecostal church as of 1952, Speck melded Christian theology and Kwakiutl culture in paintings that were promoted by Vancouver art dealer Gyula Mayer in 1961. Also a carver, Speck proceeded to exhibit at the Simon Fraser University Museum of Archaeology and Ethnology, the Meadowland Park Shopping Centre in Edmonton, and the Provincial Museum in Victoria. The Glenbow Museum in Calgary has more than two hundred watercolours by Speck. His work has also been collected by the National Museum of Man, the Museum of Anthropology, the Campbell River Museum and the San Diego Museum of Man. Speck's Kwakiutl name, Ozistalis, means "the greatest." James Speck died on May 27, 1971.

NORVAL MORRISSEAU

Norval Morrisseau has been called the "Picasso of the North" and the greatest painter that Canada has ever produced. Because of the Ojibway spirituality in his work, he is seldom considered as a British Columbian despite several decades of residency in the province.

Born March 14, 1932, on the Sand Point Ojibwe Reserve, near Beardmore, Ontario, Norval Morrisseau received his name Ahneesheenahpay, meaning Copper Thunderbird, after his mother took him to a Medicine Woman for treatment of a fever. Some elders argued he was not yet worthy of such a powerful name, but he recovered and was introduced to Ojibway shamanism by his grandfather.

Raised mainly by his grandparents, Morrisseau was sexually abused at a Roman Catholic boarding school and hospitalized with tuberculosis in the 1950s. While afflicted with TB, he began drawing and painting his visions on birch bark and paper bags. In the 1960s he travelled to Aboriginal communities in Canada and northern Minnesota, gathering more knowledge from community elders, and strengthening himself as an artist and a shaman. Founder of the Woodland School or style of painting, also known as Legend Art or Medicine Art, Morrisseau is an astral traveller who paints his visions, depicting the stories and legends of the Ojibways that were previously transmitted

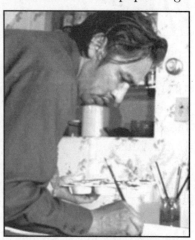

Norval Morrisseau

orally. Morrisseau's paintings are typically signed "Copper Thunderbird" using Cree syllabics taught to him by a Cree wife.

In 1962, Toronto gallery owner Jack Pollock met Morrisseau while travelling through northern Ontario and soon afterwards held Morrisseau's first one-man show in Toronto. All his paintings sold the first day. With Carl Ray, a Cree apprentice and friend from Sandy Lake, Morrisseau painted the large mural for the Natives of Canada Pavilion at Expo 67 in Montreal. Almost killed in a Vancouver hotel fire in 1972, he recovered from burns and adopted Christian beliefs that were reflected in his art. A recipient of the Order of Canada in 1978, he has had a profound influence on the work of Canadian Aboriginal artists, particularly Daphne Odjig, Jackson Beardy and Joshim Kakegamic. In 2000, Morrisseau was honoured at the En'owkin Centre in Penticton as "the bridge between traditional art and modern western painting."

Estranged from his family, he has been a cocaine addict and an alcoholic for much of his life, living on the streets in Vancouver in the late 1980s and early 1990s until he moved to Nanaimo under the care of Gabor Vadas, a former street kid who met Morrisseau in Vancouver in 1987. The relationship of Vadas and Morrisseau is featured in a CBC Life & Times documentary *A Separate Reality: The Life and Times of Norval Morrisseau* (2005). "Morrisseau was committed, from the very start, to preserving the stories and myths of his people," says writer/director Paul Carvalho. "He never wavered. As troubled as his life was, he also went through it with this incredible sense of mission."

With the companionship of Gabor Vadas and his wife, Morrisseau stopped drinking in 1991 (and got a new set of teeth), but he suffered a stroke in 1996 and has not painted since 2000. Afflicted with Parkinson's disease, he lives in a Nanaimo care facility, confined to a wheelchair. The Bau-Xi Gallery in Vancouver had a solo exhibition of Morrisseau's work in 1974 and he was the only Canadian painter invited to participate at the French Revolution bicentennial "Magicians of the Earth" exhibition at the Pompideau Museum in Paris in 1989. Morrisseau was inducted in abstentia into Thunder Bay's Walk of Fame in 2004 and his work will be the subject of a National Gallery retrospective in 2006.

As an author, Morrisseau provided illustrations for *Windigo and Other Tales of the Ojibways* (1969) but few books have been published due largely to difficulties negotiating business terms. Other Morrisseau titles are *Legends of My People: The Great Ojibway* (1965) and *Travels to the House of Invention* (1997). The latter was revised and reissued as *Norval Morrisseau: Return to the House of Invention* (2005). His former manager Jack Pollock co-edited *The Art of Norval Morrisseau* (1979) with Lister Sinclair.

SARAIN STUMP

S arain Stump's only book, *There Is My People Sleeping* (1970), was described for marketing purposes as the Ethnic Poem-Drawings of Sarain Stump, but its minimal text mainly consists of notes that served as captions. Dedicated to Mrs. George Chattaway of the Bar-S ranch "who has always been interested in the art and welfare of my people," the drawings and fractured narrative reflect a yearning for a reprieve from suffering and subjugation. "Sometimes I'd like to fall asleep, too," he writes, "close my eyes on everything."

Stump was a Cree-Shoshone artist born in 1945 on the Shoshone Reservation near Fremont, Wyoming. He received the name Sock-a-jaw-wu, meaning "the one who pulls the boat." Stump began drawing at an early age by using grocery papers and watching other Aboriginal artists.

After he moved to the Bar-S ranch in Alberta in 1964, he accumulated a collection of original drawings and commentaries that he brought with him to Vancouver Island. Sidney-based publisher Gray Campbell, also from Alberta, had had considerable success promoting George Clutesi, so he took a calculated gamble that Stump's work was also saleable. He produced three printings of Stump's book.

Sarain Stump

Some artwork by Sarain Stump and George Clutesi can now be found among the papers of Gray Campbell at the University of Victoria's Special Collections.

Despite a lack of formal training, Stump became the director of the Art Department for an Indian art program in

Saskatoon in December of 1972. As a teacher, Stump stressed awareness of Aboriginal history to his students and keenly promoted pride in Aboriginal culture. A member of the American Indian Art Historic Society and co-editor of the *Weewish Tree* magazine, Stump exhibited his carvings and paintings in Banff, Wyoming, Montreal, Calgary and the Royal Ontario Museum. He also portrayed a half-breed scout in the film *Alien Thunder* produced in Saskatchewan and released in 1973.

Stump died by drowning near Mexico City on December 20, 1974. The enigmatic yearnings of his protracted writing style are haunting in retrospect.

"It's with terror, sometimes / that I hear them calling me / but it's the light skip of a cougar / detaching me from the ground / to leave me alone / with my crazy power / till I reach the sun makers / and find myself again / in a new place."

An attempt to create a Sarain Stump Award, to be presented annually "to a Canadian Indian for his achievement in poetry," was made with the release of *Many Voices* (J.J. Douglas, 1977), an anthology of Canadian Aboriginal poetry edited by David Day and Marilyn Bowering, but this initiative was short-lived.

$2.95

THERE
IS
MY
PEOPLE
SLEEPING

Sarain
Stump

DAPHNE ODJIG

"I've jumped a lot of barriers—discrimination—and I've
fought all these things, and they are no big issue any longer."
—DAPHNE ODJIG, *EQUINOX* MAGAZINE

Like her fellow artist Norval Morrisseau, Daphne Odjig Beavon is seldom identified as a British Columbian even though she based her studio, since the late 1970s, in Anglemont, a resort town on Shuswap Lake. Recently she moved to Penticton. Similarly, as a visual artist, she is rarely recognized as an author of *Tales of the Nanabush: Books of Indian Legends for Children* (1971), *A Paintbrush in my Hand* (1993) and *Odjig: The Art of Daphne Odjig, 1985–2000* (2000).

Born on September 11, 1919, on the Wikwemikong Indian Reserve on Manitoulin Island, Manitoba, Daphne Odjig was the oldest child of a prosperous dairy farmer Dominique Odjig and his English war bride Joyce Peacy. As a mixed-race child of Potawatomi, Odawa and English descent, she overcame rheumatic fever and received her introduction in art and sketching from her grandfather who was a carver of tombstones on the reserve. Essentially self-taught, she never returned to school after she assumed the job of caring for her ill mother.

Upon the death of both her mother and grandfather in 1938, Odjig was taken to live in Parry Sound, off the reserve, at age eighteen by her disapproving English grandmother. "I learned that my people were known as boozers, lazy, not overly bright and not very dependable," she later recalled. "I began to worry about the colour of my skin." She began to use the name Fisher, an English translation of her Odawa name Odjig. With the onset of World War II she found work in a Toronto munitions factory,

When Daphne Odjig's paintings were exhibited in a Winnipeg gallery in 1977, the vice squad objected to the size of the genitals in some of the illustrations.

then she came to British Columbia where she married Paul Somerville. They had two sons.

Remaining in B.C. after her husband's death in a motorcycle accident in 1960, Odjig became a fruit farmer, growing strawberries in the Fraser Valley, and painting in the evenings. In 1963 she married Chester Beavon. They moved to northern Manitoba in 1965. Increasingly troubled by the plight of the Cree, Odjig expressed some of her anguish in her paintings, most notably *Conflict Between Good and Evil* and *The Eternal Struggle*.

Her work was noticed by Winnipeg collector Herbert Schwarz, who had collaborated with the artist Norval Morrisseau to record Ojibway legends. Odjig subsequently collaborated with Schwarz for *Tales of the Nanabush*, a collection of ten stories for children. Some of these stories about Nanabush, a trickster figure in Ojibway culture, have been reprinted as individual volumes.

In addition, Odjig's work was presented at the Winnipeg Art Gallery in 1972 alongside work by Jackson Beardy and Alex Janvier. This exhibition has been described as the first time Aboriginal artists were featured in a Canadian public art gallery, rather than a museum.

Odjig's cubistic approach to Aboriginal subject matter gained increasing favour in the 1970s after her commissioned painting "Earth Mother" was displayed at Expo 70 in Japan. In 1976, she and Beavon sold their little gallery in Winnipeg and returned to British Columbia. While living in Anglemont, she initially rented a nearby house for her studio, then built a studio where she began to undertake paintings on a much larger scale.

After her work was acclaimed at the National Arts Centre in 1978, Odjig became well-known across the country. In the 1970s she also co-founded the Professional Native Indian Artists Inc., created Indian Prints of Canada, Inc. and the Warehouse Gallery, and consulted for the Society of Canadian Artists of Native Ancestry (SCANA). Co-founded in 1972, the Professional Native Indian Artists Association has been called the "Indian Group of Seven." It consisted of Odjig, Jackson Beardy, Carl Ray, Joseph Sanchez, Eddy Cobiness, Norval Morrisseau and Alex Janvier.

Critics have long associated Odjig's art with the New Woodland School, first attributed to Norval Morrisseau, but Odjig has resisted this classification, saying her work incorporates the importance of womanhood and family, that it has strong elements of cubism, and is not wholly concerned with sacred pictography and spiritual quests.

Once referred to as a "remarkable artist" by Pablo Picasso, Odjig has received honorary degrees from Laurentian University (1982), the University of Toronto (1985), Nipissing University (1996) and Okanagan University College (2002). In 1986, she became one of four artists to be chosen by curators of the Picasso Museum in Antibes, France, to paint a memorial to Picasso. Odjig received the Order of Canada (1986) and was elected to the Royal Canadian Academy (of Art) in 1989. In 1998, near the end of her painting career, she accepted a National Aboriginal Achievement Award for Arts and Culture. Odjig has also been honoured as an Elder and presented with a sacred eagle feather by the Ojibway, whose culture is the source of inspiration for her work.

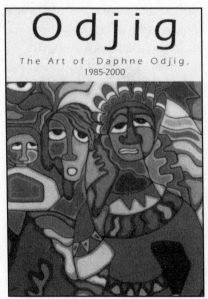

Odjig

The Art of Daphne Odjig, 1985-2000

BILL REID

"The Haida live their lives, I live mine."—BILL REID

Bill (William Ronald) Reid was primarily known as one of North America's foremost Aboriginal carvers although he was also an accomplished writer. In 1995 he was paid $3 million by the Vancouver International Airport Authority for a second version of the *Spirit of Haida Gwaii*, the jade sculpture that resides at the Canadian Embassy in Washington, D.C.

Bill Reid's mother Sophie was a Haida from Skidegate and his father Billy Reid was a naturalized Canadian of Scottish and German ancestry. They were married in 1919 and soon estranged. Reid was born on January ary 12, 1920, and grew up in Victoria with his sister Peggy. Raised by his mother, he also spent some time in the Alaska border town of Hyder where his father owned and operated several hotels. After age thirteen, Bill Reid never saw his father again.

In 1943, Reid visited his mother's hometown of Skidegate where he watched his maternal grandfather, Charles Gladstone, using silver

Bill Reid making his "plague of locusts" speech at the BC Book Prizes, 1985

and argillite to produce traditional Haida motifs. Gladstone had learned his craftsmanship from his uncle Charles Edenshaw (1839–1920), one of the greatest of Haida carvers.

Bill Reid began his first career as a radio broadcaster at CBC at age eighteen. Having moved to Toronto in 1948 to work as a radio scriptwriter, he noticed an advertisement for classes in making jewellery at the Ryerson Institute of Technology. His subsequent training in making silver and gold jewellery and engraving led him to a greater interest in Haida art, particularly the work of Charles Edenshaw, whose sister was his great-grandmother.

Reid returned to Vancouver in 1951 and opened a small jewellery workshop in a basement. His sideline career as an artist received a boost in 1957 when Provincial Museum curator Wilson Duff introduced him to carver Mungo Martin who, in turn, introduced him to wood carving. Under Martin's direction, Bill Reid carved his first totem pole in 1957, but Reid later claimed Martin was not his mentor.

Mungo Martin in 1949

Bill Reid quit the CBC and worked with Kwakiutl carver Doug Cranmer (who had been staying at Mungo Martin's house in Victoria) from 1958 to 1962 helping to construct a portion of a Haida village at UBC, at the invitation of Harry Hawthorn, and also repairing totem poles in Stanley Park. He later trained at the Central School of Art and Design in London and accepted a commission for Expo 67 in

Bill Reid's Spirit of Haida Gwaii *carving is featured on the Canadian $20 bill.*

Montreal. He carved a 78-foot red cedar totem for the Skidegate Band office in 1978.

Bill Reid gained increasingly prestigious and lucrative commissions and received honorary degrees from six universities. His best-known works include the *Spirit of Haida Gwaii,* a pair of 19-foot canoes, one at the Vancouver International Airport and the other at the Canadian Embassy in Washington, D.C.; the *Lord of the Under Sea,* a killer whale at the Vancouver Public Aquarium; *Raven and the First Men,* a 4.5-ton yellow cedar sculpture at UBC's Museum of Anthropology; and *Lootaas,* the Haida-style canoe that was commissioned for Expo 86.

Having contributed to the coffee table book *Islands at the Edge* (1984), Reid made an unexpected appearance at the first BC Book Prizes gala in 1985, accepting the Roderick Haig-Brown Book Prize and reminding the audience of the ravages of white civilization, calling it "the worst plague of locusts."

Bill Reid's first career as a radio announcer and scriptwriter fostered a lifelong appreciation of books and writing. *Solitary Raven: The Collected Writings of Bill Reid* (2001) reveals him as a prolific social, artistic and spiritual commentator. He provided illustrations for several books and collaborated with Bill Holm for *Indian Art on the Northwest Coast: A Dialogue on Craftsmanship and Aesthetics* (1975) and with Robert Bringhurst for *Raven Steals the Light* (1984). Reid's books also include *Out of the Silence* (1971) and *All the Gallant Beasts and Monsters* (1992).

Bill Reid died on March 13, 1998, after a 30-year struggle with Parkinson's disease. An eight-hour memorial gathering at the University of British Columbia attracted one thousand people. As Reid had requested, his ashes were interred at T'annu, a deserted village near Skidegate, where his grandmother was born.

There have been numerous critical and appreciative studies of his work including Maria Tippett's biography *Bill Reid, Becoming an Indian*, a controversial work that removed some of the scales from the eyes of those who have sought to deify Reid. On September 29, 2004, the Bank of Canada issued 25 million new $20 bank notes that feature four works by Reid, including *Raven and the First Men*.

PHIL NUYTTEN
(& ELLEN NEEL)

Phil Nuytten is a Métis who apprenticed as a carver, from age twelve, with Ellen Neel, one of the three main subjects for his book, *The Totem Carvers* (1982), a particularly well-illustrated study of the work and lives of Kwakiutl carvers Charlie James, Ellen Neel and Mungo Martin. All three carvers were related but from three different generations.

Charlie James was born in Port Townsend, Washington, around 1867, and he died in Alert Bay in 1938. His granddaughter and student Ellen May Neel was born on November 14, 1916, at Alert Bay, and she died on February 3, 1966. Her uncle Mungo Martin, step-son of Charlie James, was born at Fort Rupert around 1880, and he died in Victoria on August 16, 1962. *The Totem Carvers* is most valuable for its portrait of Ellen Neel, who pioneered commercial sales of Kwakiutl art in Vancouver—with unhappy consequences.

Fluent in English and Kwak'wala, Neel was the daughter of Charlie Newman, the son of a Kwakiutl mother and the American seaman James Newman. Her mother Lucy Lilac James was daughter of Charlie James and Sara Nina Finlay, a non-Aboriginal. Raised in Alert Bay, she married the non-Aboriginal ex-convict Ted Neel in 1939 after she had given birth to their son Dave in 1937.

The Neel family moved to Vancouver in 1943. Five more children were born by 1945. After Ted Neel, a sheet metal worker, suffered the first of a series of strokes in 1946, the Neels converted their home on Powell Street into a workshop to enable Ellen Neel to become the main breadwinner. Commissioned to produce an insignia for the Totemland Society (the brainchild of public relations man Harry Duker and Mayor Charley Thompson), Neel provided the model for the totem pole that was used on the letterhead of the society for the promotion of tourism.

Duker arranged for the Neel family to begin carving in Stanley Park where they had a tent and conducted semi-sanctioned commercial sales, eventually establishing a permanent workshop and sales site, with the formal approval of the Parks Board commissioners, at Ferguson Point, near Pauline Johnson's burial site. In 1947, Ellen Neel was interviewed by ethnographer Marius Barbeau for his monograph on Charlie James and she provided much of the information that appears in Barbeau's well-known scholarly work *Totem Poles*.

In the spring of 1948, President Norman Mackenzie of UBC bought Neel's first polished totem during a conference on Native Indian Affairs at UBC's Acadia Camp, prompting the *Vancouver Province* to describe her as "probably the only woman totem pole carver in the world." Soon thereafter her family-run Totem Art Studios provided a 16-foot thunderbird totem as a gift to the Alma Mater Society. It was presented at the UBC football stadium before 6,000 football fans by Chief William Scow of Alert Bay, president of the Native Brotherhood of B.C. and publisher of the *Native Voice* newspaper.

In full ceremonial regalia, Scow magnanimously conferred the right to use the term "Thunderbird" by UBC teams. "This is according to the laws of my people," he said, "and [the use of the name] is therefore legal for the first time."

An association with UBC led to an invitation that summer for Neel to restore four large Kwakiutl poles from Fort Rupert, one of which was carved by Charlie James 16 years before she was born, for the Department of Anthropology and its director Harry Hawthorn. As it became increasingly apparent that this work lim-

ited her tourism sales in Stanley Park, and as Hawthorn envisioned a more ambitious plan to start making copies of decaying poles, Ellen Neel asked her uncle Mungo Martin if he would undertake the UBC work on her behalf.

At age sixty-two in 1951, Martin welcomed an opportunity to employ the craftsmanship he had

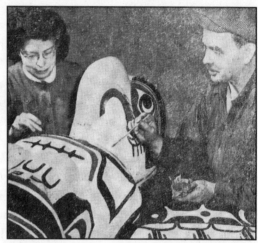

A 16-ft. totem carved by Ellen and Ted Neel (above) was presented to the UBC Alma Mater Society in 1948 by Chief William Scow, president of the Native Brotherhood, who gave permission for UBC teams to use the name Thunderbird.

learned from his step-father Charlie James, who had also taught him to read and write in a phonetic transcription of the Kwakiutl language developed by Reverend Alfred James Hall. Able to speak only rudimentary English and not highly paid for his work, Mungo Martin was nonetheless happy to live at Acadia Camp with his wife and to work fulltime for UBC, carving two original totems while making copies of others. "Mungo Martin is the most creative person I have ever known," Audrey Hawthorn enthused.

Ellen Neel increasingly turned her hand to commercial projects in the 1950s, such as providing decor for a Harrison Hot Springs hotel foyer, completing a pole for the Vancouver Tourist Association in conjunction with an American television program, and making a wedding gift for Lord and Lady Selkirk of London, England. When the Neels' family business contrived to increase production of "idiot sticks" in the early 1950s, they retained the Ferguson Point workshop for sales and developed a workshop closer to home in conjunction with their basement workshop at 348 Glen Drive.

During this period Phil Nuytten began his apprenticeship with the Neels during the summers. They supplied an eleven-foot pole to a museum in Copenhagen in 1953, the same year Mungo Martin held an auspicious potlatch in Victoria to celebrate his work at Thunderbird Park in Victoria. Although the Neel children received new Kwakiutl names during this gathering, their parents increasingly disregarded traditional values in favour of sales. At age sixteen, David Neel was encouraged to complete miniature likeness of comedian Bob Hope for the "the world's smallest totem" that was presented to Bob Hope for publicity purposes.

The family provided five poles to an Edmonton shopping centre in 1955. The children began to leave home soon thereafter. Ted and Ellen Neel moved to White Rock, B.C., in 1959, accepted an invitation to demonstrate totem pole carving at Stratford, Ontario, in 1960, and returned to B.C. to live in Aldergrove. Their eldest son David died at twenty-four in a car accident in Washington State, in September of 1961. The health of both Ellen Neel and Ted Neel declined soon afterward.

Whereas the entire family had once been able to fulfill an order from the Hudson's Bay Company for 5,000 tiny poles, she was soon reduced to signing her name to the work of others and selling her own collection of traditional art pieces, her sketch books and even her tools. She entered Vancouver General Hospital in January of 1966 and died at age forty-nine. Some of her ashes were scattered from a rented plane over Johnstone Strait and the Cluxewe River near Port McNeill; the rest were buried at Alert Bay.

Born and educated in Vancouver, Phil Nuytten was living in North Vancouver as an internationally recognized diver and innovator in the field of underwater technology when he wrote *The Totem Carvers*, the primary record of Ellen Neel's life. For later self-marketers such as Bill Reid, Robert Davidson, Roy Henry Vickers and Susan Point, Ellen Neel provided a salutary example of how not to proceed as an Aboriginal artist. High-end art galleries and commissions were preferable to department stores or tourist shops.

WILLIE SEAWEED

"Willie Seaweed was born in a cedar plank house on the shores of an inlet that knew only canoe travel . . . and by the time he died unmanned space craft were landing on the moon."—MICHAEL M. AMES

Along with his fellow Kwakiutl artists Charlie James and Mungo Martin, and Haida artist Charles Edenshaw, Willie Seaweed provided an integral cultural link with the past, during much of the twentieth century, before Aboriginal artists and their work became widely accepted.

Born in Nugent Sound in approximately 1873, Seaweed became Chief Hilamas of the Nakwaktokw (or 'Nak'waxda'xw) tribe and a proponent of the potlatch during the years it was declared an illegal activity from 1884 to 1951. He also preserved his people's traditions as a sculptor, singer and storyteller.

The surname Seaweed is reportedly derived from his Aboriginal name Siwid meaning "Many Travel by Canoe to be at His Potlatches" but it was more commonly translated as "Smoky-Top," as if to suggest a volcano.

Seaweed's carving was brought to prominence by Bill Holm with an exhibition at the Pacific Science Center in Seattle, Washington, in 1983–1984 called *Smoky-Top: The Art and Times of Willie Seaweed*. From this exhibition arose a book featuring Seaweed's

Willie Seaweed

work, *Smoky-Top, The Art and Times of Willie Seaweed* (1983), followed by *Innovations for a Changing Time: Willie Seaweed, A Master Kwakiutl Artist* (1992). Seaweed's work was later displayed at the Vancouver Art Gallery in 1998 as part of an exhibition of wooden masks called *Down from the Shimmering Sky.*

In correspondence with Wilson Duff in 1955, Seaweed once described how and when his people moved to Blunden Harbour, a place on the mainland opposite the northern end of Vancouver Island. Known to his people as Ba'as, this village became widely associated with a famous painting of its waterfront by Emily Carr. Seaweed died at Blunden Harbour in 1967. A portrait of Seaweed by Mildred Valley Thornton appears in her *Indian Lives and Legends.*

ROY HENRY VICKERS

R oy Henry Vickers was born in 1946 in Greenville, B.C. His mother Grace Freeman was a schoolteacher of Yorkshire ancestry; his father Arthur Vickers was a half-Tsimshian, half-Heiltsuk fisherman. His grandfather Henry Vickers was a Heiltsuk who left Bella Bella to marry a Tsimshian woman in Kitlatka, a small village on Dolphin Island near Prince Rupert.

Raised in Kitkatla, as well as in Hazelton and Victoria, Roy Henry Vickers graduated from Oak Bay High School in 1965. He worked as a fireman in the Victoria area before he went north to

Roy Henry Vickers

attend the Kitanmax (Gitanmaax) School of Northwest Indian Art at 'Ksan on the Skeena River.

Vickers co-founded the Northwest Native Artists Guild with Robert Davidson and Art Thompson. After ending his two-year marriage with Liane Leslie Vickers in 1978, Vickers spent two years fishing and moved to Tofino in 1980. He had his first exhibition at the Eagle Down Gallery in Edmonton, a facility that was opened in 1978 by his sister Margaret Ruth Vickers.

Vickers' first coffee table book *Solstice: The Art of Roy Vickers* (1988) was a bestseller. His second coffee table book is *Copperman: The Art of Roy Henry Vickers* (2003). He also provided 25 paintings for *The Elders Are Watching* (1990), a poetic text by Dave Bouchard.

The documentation of how Vickers carved a 30-foot Salmon Pole for the 1994 Commonwealth Games in Victoria is provided in *Spirit Transformed: A Journey from Tree to Totem* (1996), with 50 photographs by Bob Herger. It describes how Vickers transformed a majestic cedar from the Walbran Valley and also how he overcame personal demons as an alcoholic from the late 1960s until 1992, when he checked himself into an alcohol recovery clinic in Arizona.

While living on the Tsartlip Reserve near Victoria, Vickers acted as an artistic advisor for the building of Saanich Commonwealth Place and consulted on the refurbishment of the Vancouver International Airport. In 1987, at a Commonwealth Heads of Government meeting in Vancouver, the provincial government presented

Roy Vickers donated the Eagle Full Circle logo design for the BC Book Prizes.

Her Majesty Queen Elizabeth II with an original painting by Vickers entitled *A Meeting of Chiefs*. Copies of Vickers' print entitled *The Homecoming* were given to American President Bill Clinton and Soviet President Boris Yeltsin at their Vancouver summit meeting in April of 1993.

Some of Vickers' paintings have price tags of more than $30,000. His former wife tried unsuccessfully to sue him for proceeds from his art sales, partially on the grounds that she had inspired some of his work, but B.C. Supreme Court Justice Hugh Davies ruled in 1991 that the delay in her demand to enforce a 1981 settlement order was inordinate.

"Change comes from understanding ourselves," said Vickers, who converted to Christianity. "Revival, culture, heritage, environment. These are the key words for this last decade of the century." In June of 1993 he presented a traditional copper shield called a hyetsk to the chiefs of the Heilsuk First Nation in Bella Bella. Now living at Brentwood Bay near Victoria, he built Tofino's Eagle Aerie Gallery in 1986 and the Roy Henry Vickers Gallery in Brentwood Bay in 1999.

ROBERT DAVIDSON

"I started out wanting to be a contemporary artist, but then I found I was a contemporary Haida artist." —ROBERT DAVIDSON

Born in Hydaberg, Alaska, on November 4, 1946, and raised at Masset on Haida Gwaii, Robert Davidson is the son of Claude Davidson, a carver, and grandson of Robert Davidson, Sr., a carver and a hereditary chief from the town of Kayung. He is also related to legendary Haida carvers Charles Edenshaw and Albert Edward Edenshaw through his grandmother Florence Edenshaw.

Robert Davidson

As one of B.C.'s most successful Aboriginal artists, Robert Davidson has had his work celebrated in *Robert Davidson: Eagle of the Dawn* (1993), edited by Ian M. Thom in conjunction with a major exhibit at the Vancouver Art Gallery, as well as *Eagle Transforming: The Art of Robert Davidson* (1994).

Davidson moved to Vancouver in 1965 and apprenticed for 18 months with Bill Reid after Reid discovered Davidson conducting a carving demonstration at a Vancouver department store. When he carved his first totem pole in Masset in 1969, it was the first to be raised in Masset for more than 90 years. Davidson has since erected poles in New York, Dublin, Montreal and Toronto. He supplied a pole for the headquarters of Maclean-Hunter in Toronto; the Pepsi Cola company commissioned three poles called *Three Variations on Killer Whale Myths* in 1986 for its international sculpture park outside New York City.

Multi-talented, Davidson has worked with argillite, gold, silver and wood, carving masks and making jewellery, when not undertaking monumental works. He also made the talking stick that was presented to Pope John Paul II in Vancouver in 1984.

MICHAEL NICOLL YAHGULANAAS

Illustrated with his own Japanese-style cartoons, Michael Nicoll Yahgulanaas' *The Last Voyage of the Black Ship* (2002) is a mythical history of civilization, logging and rainforest ecosystems. The Black Ship represents the British Columbia logging industry and its failure to understand the "Haida Brave." In the story a sleeping spirit named Pink Gyrri is awakened and tries to save Mother Earth. In *A Tale of Two Shamans* (2001), the artist also rc-interpreted the Haida story about two brothers travelling to and from the Spirit World, incorporating versions from different dialects.

Michael Nicoll Yahgulanaas, self-portrait

As a cartoonist, he has challenged stereotypes in publications that include *Tales of Raven Vol. 1* "No Tankers Tanks" (1977); *Tales of Raven Vol. 2* "Mutants of the Pit" (1987); *Spruceroots* magazine (1998–2002); *Nonni's Will* (2002); *Vancouver Special Anthology* (2002); *What Right! Anthology* (2002); *Madburger* (2002); *Redwire* (2003); and *Crank* magazine (2003).

SUSAN POINT

Born in Alert Bay in 1952, Susan Point is one of the few female carvers of Aboriginal art and one of the most successful Aboriginal artists of British Columbia. Point grew up on the Musqueam Band reserve, near the mouth of the Fraser River, until she was sent to the Sechelt residential school at age nine and kept away from her family for five years. She worked in a cannery with her mother until moving to various secretarial positions. In 1981, at the age of twenty-nine, Point enrolled in a six-week jewellery-making course at Vancouver Community College. Later Michael Kew, a UBC anthropologist, helped Point learn about her Coast Salish artistic heritage.

Point has had her work in dozens of exhibitions since 1982 and received an honorary doctorate from the University of Victoria in 2000. There have been numerous publications in association with her exhibitions, as well as a book edited by Gary Wyatt, *Susan Point: Coast Salish Artist* (2000), published to coincide with

Susan Point at the National Museum of the American Indian at the Smithsonian Institute

a Vancouver exhibition of her work ranging from jewellery and prints to monumental sculpture. Each is accompanied by a statement from Point.

"Coast Salish art," she has written, "is relatively unknown to most people today as it was an almost lost art after European contact—the reason being is that Salish lands were the first to be settled by the Europeans which adversely affected my people's traditional life cycle. . . ."

The sacred and private character of an image revealed in dreams or visions—either threatening or beneficial—is an integral part of Coast Salish heritage. Frogs are important symbols for Point as a memory of childhood when the Musqueam people would listen for the singing of frogs as a sign of coming spring. One of her pieces, "Singing the Season," shows five carved frogs with silver domes for eyes.

Susan Point often works on large-scale productions, in collaboration with architects, including a major installation of house posts to welcome visitors at the Vancouver International Airport.

VICKIE JENSEN PHOTO

Mary Johnson of Kispiox

IV
ALSO NOTEWORTHY

ANTOINE, Irene: Along with Catherine Bird, **Ileen Heer**, Mildred Martin and Florence Sam, Irene Antoine co-authored *Nak'al Bun Whudakelhne Bughuni* (1991), a bilingual classroom dictionary for and about the people of Stuart Lake. The project was conceived and managed by Ileen Heer, a classroom teacher in Fort St. James. It is the second dictionary for the Central Carrier people, following the *Central Carrier Bilingual Dictionary* published in 1974.

ARCHIBALD, Jo-ann: The director of the UBC First Nations House of Learning from 1993 to 2001, Jo-ann Archibald of the Stó:lo Nation became an editor of the *Canadian Journal of Native Education* and received a National Aboriginal Achievement Award in 2000 for her work in education. With the House of Learning's first director Verna Kirkness, Archibald co-authored *The First Nations Longhouse: Our Home Away From Home* (2001).

ARIMA, E.Y.: Nuu-chah-nulth elders and ethnographers gathered oral history for *Between Ports Alberni and Renfrew: Notes on West Coast Peoples* (1991) by Arima, **Louis Clamhouse**, **Joshua Edgar**, Charles Jones, **Denis St. Claire** and **John Thomas**.

BLACKSTOCK, Michael: Gitxsan Michael Blackstock of Kamloops is a forester and mediator whose *Faces in the Forest* (2001) examines tree art in conjunction with First Nations cosmology, citing trees within Gitxsan, Nisga'a, Tlingit, Carrier and Déné territories. He also self-published *Salmon Run: A Florilegium of Aboriginal Ecological Poetry* (2005), commentaries that incorporate the trickster perspective of Wyget the Raven.

BORROWS, John: Having gained the first of his five academic degrees in 1987, Anishinabe lawyer John Borrows of the Nawash First Nation became the Law Foundation Chair in Aboriginal Justice at the University of Victoria Faculty of Law in 2001. He is the author of *Recovering Canada: The Resurgence of Indigenous Law* (2002), for which he won the Donald Smiley Award for the best book in Canadian Political Science, as well as *Aboriginal Law: Cases,*

Materials and Commentary (1998). Borrows was the first academic Director of First Nations Legal Studies at the University of British Columbia and he founded the Intensive Program in Lands, Resources and First Nations Governments at Osgoode Hall Law School. He has taught more than 400 Aboriginal law students and helped initiate the June Callwood Program in Aboriginal Law at the University of Toronto. He received a National Aboriginal Achievement Award in the category of Law and Justice in 2002.

BOYD, Laura Marie: A Nazko band member who teaches the Dakelh language, Boyd published a story about a young girl and her grandmother gathering food in a traditional way in *'Utsoo and I (Si' ink'ez' Utsoo)* (1990). This story in Ulkatcho Carrier and English contains a recipe for nawus (Indian ice-cream) and was translated from English by Janie Jack, Bella Leon, Gertie Leon, Mack Squinas, Rose Squinas, Jimmy Stillas, Leona Toney and Jennifer West. Boyd's other books for children are *My Home Forever* (1989) and *For Someone Special* (1990). She received her B.A. in First Nations Studies from the University of Northern British Columbia in 1998.

BROOKS, Cheryl: Of Stó:lo ancestry, activist Cheryl Brooks co-edited (with Doreen Jensen) *In Celebration of our Survival: The First Nations of British Columbia* (1991), a collection of writings and art that appeared as a special issue (No. 89) of *BC Studies.*

CAFFEY, John: John Caffey and others prepared a grade seven text about the 17 Secwepemc bands for *Shuswap History: The First 100 Years of Contact* (1990).

CALIHOO, Robert: At age ten Robert Calihoo was living in Edmonton as Robert Royer when he discovered he was an adopted Aboriginal. He found his father Albert Calihoo and went to live with their relatives on a reserve. Calihoo later worked as manager for the Nimpkish Band Council at Alert Bay prior to co-writing his memoir with Robert Hunter, *Occupied Canada: A Young White Man Discovers His Unsuspected Past (1991)*, which earned a Governor General's Award for Non-Fiction in 1992.

CAMPBELL, Nicola I. Raised in B.C.'s Nicola Valley, Nicola I. Campbell is a UBC Fine Arts student of Interior Salish and Métis ancestry. Illustrated by Kim LaFave, her first children's book *Shi-shi-etko* (2005) portrays a young girl named Shi-shi-etko ("she loves to play in the water") who must leave her family to attend a residential school. She spends her remaining four days playing outside and listening to her parents' and grandparents' teachings, intent on keeping everything inside her "bag of memories."

CHARLEYBOY, Orrey: Orrey Charleyboy wrote *Tsi Del Del: Redstone* (1991), a local history produced from Williams Lake. The Tsi Del Del First Nation at Alexis Creek is also known as the Redstone Band. The Charleyboy family is prominent in the West Chilcotin where Chief Ervin Charleyboy helped introduce the first annual Tsi Del Del rodeo with Steve Horsman, Ervin Charleyboy, Joyce and Gene Cooper, Edna Lulua, Seraphine and Dixie William, Geraldine Solomon and Marilyn Charleyboy in 1998.

COHEN, Bill: An En'owkin Centre graduate, Okanagan artist and teacher Bill Cohen has explored and recorded the "Indian Cowboy" tradition of Aboriginal ranching and rodeos in the Okanagan territory that stretches across the 49th parallel. Included in his *Stories and Images of What the Horse Has Done For Us* (1998) are photographs from the late nineteenth-century onwards. He also illustrated Ellen White's *Kwulasulwut II* (1997) and Jordan Wheeler's *Chuck in the City* (2000), two children's books.

COLLINS, Theo: As an Aboriginal law student at the University of British Columbia, Theo Collins prepared a layman's 35-page guide to the Sechelt Indian Band Self-Government Act of 1986 entitled *The Sechelt Act and What It Means* (1988).

VICKIE JENSEN PHOTO

Margaret Cook during canning season

COOK, Margaret: Known as Ada ("mother") to generations at Alert Bay, Margaret Cook was born on Turnour Island and grew up in a Big House before attending St. Michael's Residential School. She served as linguistic informant for the *Learning Kwak'wala* (1980–1981) series of language and culture materials. The CD-ROM *Nugwa'am* (2000) produced by the U'Mista Cultural Society, was dedicated to the memory of Agnes Cranmer and Margaret Cook. They were both involved in the Anglican Church at Alert Bay.

COURTOREILLE, Fred & Mary: Fred and Mary Courtoreille's memories of bush life and residential school in northeastern B.C. between 1910 and 1930 are recorded in *Roast Moose & Rosaries: Fred & Mary's Story* (1997), co-written with Terrance Armstrong and prepared by the Muskoti Learning Centre.

CRANMER, Agnes: Agnes Cranmer (neé Hunt) of Alert Bay carried the name G̱wanti'lakw meaning "born to be heavy" (referring to wealth). Franz Boas stayed at her house on one of his visits. Later, Agnes Cranmer and her first cousin Nunu (Helen Knox) gave Boas' descendants, Norman and Doris Boas, names at a potlatch. Agnes Cramner taught traditional

VICKIE JENSEN PHOTO

Agnes Cranmer teaching traditional dancing at 'Namgis Band School dancing for many years at the 'N̲amgis Band School and served as a resource consultant for the *Learning Kwak'wala* series (1980–1981) and for its accompanying teacher-training program. One of her daughters is Gloria Cranmer Webster.

CUTHAND, Beth: Cree Beth Cuthand teaches at the Nicola Valley Institute of Technology in Merritt. Her poetry books are *Horse Dance to Emerald Mountain* (1987) and *Voices in the Waterfall* (1989);

Earl Einarson

her bilingual children's book, in Cree and English, is *The Little Duck/Sikihpsis* (1999). She co-edited *Reinventing the Enemy's Language* (1997) and *Gatherings, Volume V* (1994).

EINARSON, Earl: A member of the Ktunaxa First Nation of the Columbia and Kootenay Rivers region, Earl Einarson wrote *The Moccasins* (2004), an autobiographical children's story about a foster child who has a positive experience when his foster mother gives him a gift of moccasins and encourages him to take pride in his heritage. Illustrated by Penticton's Julie Flett, of Cree/Métis descent, this story was shortlisted for a BC Book Prize.

FELIX, Dolly: Dolly Felix narrated her version of a Stó:lo story for *The Hunter and the Sasquatch* (1981). Also known as Sophie Joe, storyteller Dolly Felix was an assistant to Andy Paull during his involvement with the Indian Brotherhood. Born on October 19, 1897, she first lived with her parents Sophie and James Johnson at the mouth of the Harrison River before moving to Nicomen Island in 1902. At age eleven she stopped attending St. Mary's Residential School in Mission. She married Richard (Dick) Joe from Chehalis in 1923. She had twelve children and at least 35

Felix Dolly

great-grandchildren. As a member of the Coqualeetza Elders Group in 1981, she was assisted by Laverne Adams (text) and Peter Lindley (illustrations).

GAWA, Edith: Edith Gawa taught Gitksan in the Kispiox school for many years and collaborated with Jay Powell and Vickie Jensen for *Gitxsanimix for Kids* (1978), a series of books that has been used in schools for the eastern Gitksan dialect area. A chieftainess of the Frog Clan at Kispiox, she was severely injured when struck by an automobile in the late 1970s and retired from teaching.

GUERIN, Arnold: Arnold Guerin was a pioneer in the movement to revitalize the Aboriginal languages in B.C. He taught one of the first school-based courses and his *Hunq'umi'num Language: Book 1* (1993) set the standard for Aboriginal language primers. A member of the Musqueam Band, he taught on the Cooper Island Reserve and then in Musqueam. He also served as a resource for UBC linguistic field methods courses and collaborated

Edith Gawa

with Wayne Suttles in producing a grammar and dictionary. Born "before World War I," he died in the mid-1980s.

HALE, Janet Campbell: Lawyer Janet Campbell Hale wrote a 205-page resource guide for identifying and treating addictive behaviour among Aboriginal youth, *Native Students with Problems of Addiction* (1990). The work was annotated by Don Sawyer of the Native Adult Education Resource Centre in Salmon Arm.

HAMILTON, Ron: Born in 1948, Nuu-chah-nulth ethnographer Ron Hamilton contributed the introduction and 14 drawings to the first cooperatively written product of the Barkley Sound Language Development Project, the *Nuu-chah-nulth Phrase Book & Dictionary: Barkley Sound Dialect* (2004), designed and typeset by Maggie Paquet of Port Alberni. The Language Development Team of Hilda Nookemis, Deborah Cook and Denny Durocher worked for 18 months with representatives from the Huu-ay-aht, Ucluelet, Toquaht and Uchucklesaht First Nations to produce the 192-page, pocket-sized book in an effort to revive a rarely spoken language. Ron Hamilton also provided illustrations for his uncle Peter Webster's autobiography *As Far As I Know: Reminiscences of an Ahousat Elder* (1983).

HANNA, Darwin & HENRY, Mamie: With the accompaniment of Lytton Indian Band elder Mamie Henry as his translator, UBC law student and Lytton Indian Band member Darwin Hanna tracked down Thompson (Nlha7kapmx) elders in the Fraser Canyon and Nicola Valley in 1993 and tape recorded their stories for *Our Tellings: Interior Salish Stories of the Nlha7kapmx People* (1995). Hanna received some encouragement and advice from Wendy Wickwire, whom he met while working with the Stein Valley Rediscovery Program, as well as directions from his uncle Nathan Spinks. Co-author Mamie Henry was one of the first to develop a writing system for the Nlha7kapmx language and teach it in schools. Their collaboration includes creation and non-creation stories, as well as some photos of the informants: Phil Acar,

Hilda Austin, Fred Bea, Marion Bent, Peter Bob, Christine Bobb, Mandy Brown, Tom George, Herbert (Buddy) Hanna, Fred Hanna, Walter Isaac, Anthony Joe, Mable Joe, Herb Manuel, Edna Malloway, Mildred Mitchell, Louie Phillips, Bert Seymour, Rosie Skuki, Nathan Spinks, Dorothy Ursaki, Bill Walkem, Mary Williams and Annie York.

HARRIS, Heather: A Cree-Métis who teaches in the First Nations Studies program at the University of Northern British Columbia, Heather Harris is also a poet, jeweller, clothing designer and traditional dancer who gathered her often humorous poetry for *Rainbow Dancer* (1999). Formerly married to Gitxsan chief David Harris, she participates in Rainbow Dancing with her daughters and credits Mary Johnson (Antgwulilibiksxw) as "the most knowledgeable lady I ever knew."

Celina Harry

HARRY, Celina: Having taught Shuswap language and culture in her local elementary school at Alkali Lake, Celina Harry co-authored *Let's Study Shuswap, Books 1-2* (1977, 1980) and provided input for the *Shuswap Teachers Manual* (1983).

HART, Jim: Along with his fellow Haida carver **Reg Davidson**, carver, goldsmith and painter Jim Hart produced *Haida Artifacts: An Exhibition* (1990). In 1999, Hart received his name 7idansuu (pronounced "ee-dan-soo") as an Eagle Clan hereditary chief. It was once held by Charles Edenshaw. In 2003 he installed *The Three Watchmen*, a 14-foot bronze sculpture at the entrance to an apartment residence in Kerrisdale's Quilchena Park in Vancouver. After two years of work on the project, Hart supervised the casting process at the Tallix Art Foundry in Beacon, New York. Hart, who lives in Masset, received the Order of British Columbia in 2003.

HUNGRY WOLF, Beverly: Born on the Blood Indian Reserve in southern Alberta, Beverly Hungry Wolf was raised in a large family, attended boarding school and met her Swiss-born husband at a powwow in Montana. For many years they raised a family in Skookumchuck, B.C., where they operated their own publishing imprint, Good Medicine Books, and collaborated on numerous titles about Blackfoot culture.

Beverly Hungry Wolf

They have since parted company. Beverly Hungry Wolf is the author of *The Ways of my Grandmother* (1980) and *Daughters of the Buffalo Women: Maintaining the Tribal Faith* (1996). Both reflect the stories and wisdom of her mother Ruth Little Bear and her female ancestors and elders.

IRONSTAND, Raphael: Raised in bleak circumstances on a reserve in Manitoba, Raphael Ironstand, a Métis, stowed away in a truck at age nine to accompany other children to a residential school. There he was taunted as "Monias" (white man in Cree) for having light skin. Later, upon reading a copy of Stewart Dickson's *Broken Wing*, a novel about a bush pilot in northern B.C., Ironstand was inspired to get in touch with Dickson, who was living in Gibsons, B.C. Together they produced *Hey Monias! The Story of Raphael Ironstand* (1993). Ironstand was living in Nanaimo when his memoir was published.

JACK, Agness: Active in the Cariboo Tribal Council, Agness Jack of the Shuswap First Nation edited testimonials from 32 individuals about their experiences within the Kamloops Indian Residential School that operated from 1893 to 1979. The recollections in *Behind Closed Doors: Stories from the Kamloops Indian Residential School (2001)* were compiled by the Secwepemc Cultural Education Society as part of a community healing project.

JACOBSON, Diane: Diane "Honey" Jacobson's memories of communal living in Alert Bay, within a large Kwakiutl family, are the focus for *My Life in a Kwag'ul Big House* (2005), a yearning for bygone days. Jacobson is a 'Namgis First Nation member with family ties to the Mowachaht and the Mamalilakala (Mamalilaculla) settlement on Village Island. Alert Bay, located on Cormorant Island off the east coast of Vancouver Island, was one of the best-known Aboriginal villages on the B.C. coast, popular with Edwardian tourists, after the Union Steamship Company commenced service to the community in 1896. The settlement arose after two Nimpkish River settlers established a salmon saltery there around 1870. The Fort Rupert Anglican mission relocated there in 1878 and a new cannery and sawmill attracted 'Namgis families from the Nimpkish Valley in the 1880s. The town was named for the British warship HMS *Alert* that conducted coastal surveys.

JOHN, Gracie: With consultation from Mary John, Sr., Veronica George, Fraser Alexis, Celina John and linguist Dick Walker, Gracie John & **Mary John, Jr.,** produced *Saik'uz Whut'enne Hubughunek* (1991), an Elementary Central Carrier bilingual dictionary to accompany *Nak'al Bun Whudakelhne Bughuni*. It contains an Athapaskan dialect map, keys to pronunciation and simple sentences for classroom use. The dictionaries were produced by the Yinka Déné Language Institute (Edward John, president) in association with the Carrier Linguistic Committee (Ray Prince, president).

JOHNSON, Mary: Carrying a chief's title from one of the houses in the Fireweed Clan, Gitksan elder Mary Johnson of Kispiox was instrumental in bringing people together in support of the concept of 'Ksan Village. Fluent in English and Gitxsanimx, she co-authored the *Gitxsanimx for Kids series, Books 1–7* (1977–1980).

JOSEPH, Gene: Gene Joseph produced *Sharing the Knowledge: A First Nations Resource Guide* (1992) for the Legal Services Society (Theresa Tait, director, Native Programs). Although this resource guide is chiefly concerned with Aboriginal self-determination and legal rights, the bibliographic survey for its opening history and culture section is broad. The second section concerns issues such as environmental protection, constitutional matters and Aboriginal title. A brief third section cites sources for considering the future. Several hundred titles are listed for reference.

KEW, Della: Musqueam Della Kew is credited as the editor of a re-issued version of anthropologist Pliney Earle Goddard's 1924 work, *Indian Art and Culture of the Northwest Coast* (1974). Additional artwork was gathered from sources that included *Those Born at Koona* by John and Carolyn Smyly, and *Artifacts of the Northwest Coast Indians* by Hilary Stewart.

KOON, Danny: As a young member of the Kwiksutaneuk Band, Danny Koon of Alert Bay published a slim and rare collection of drawings in an untitled book format in 1971.

LOUIS, Shirley: Okanagan band member Shirley Louis researched family trees and collected interviews with elders for *Q'Sapi: A History of Okanagan People as Told by Okanagan Families* (2002). *Q'Sapi* means "long time ago." Her anthology provides documentation of Okanagan Indian Band veterans who served in World Wars I and II and suggests the Interior Salish were matrilineal. Archaeological evidence of indigenous people living in the Okanagan Valley corridor dates as far back as 6500 B.C.

MARSDEN, Solomon: Deeply committed to cultural maintenance

VICKIE JENSEN PHOTO

Solomon Marsden being interviewed by Jay Powell

and revitalization, Solomon Marsden was a chieftain and clan leader at Gitanyow (Kitwancool). He served as Gitksan language editor of the *Learning Gitksan* (Western dialect) series of school books produced in the late 1970s in conjunction with Jay Powell and Vickie Jensen, a Vancouver couple who spent their summers living in Kispiox and/or Kitwancool over a five-year period. With the collaboration of Marsden and others, they produced *Learning Gitksan, Books 2, 3* and *4* (1980) and a host of other learning materials.

MCIVOR, Dorothy: As someone who experienced life within the largest Protestant Indian residential school in Canada, at Sardis, B.C., Dorothy Matheson McIvor wrote *Coqualeetza "Vestiga Nulla Retrosum" (No Backward Step)* (1978).

MICHELL, Teresa: Teresa Michell wrote two children's books, *The Mischievous Cubs* (1981) and *How the Coho Got his Hooked Nose* (1981), both from the Coqualeetza Education Training Centre in Sardis, formerly a residential school.

NAPOLEON, Art: Produced for and by Aboriginals, Cree educator Art Napoleon's *Native Studies of North Eastern B.C.* (1991) incorporates information from Beaver First Nation elders for an overview of pre-contact, contact and colonization, and contemporary periods.

PATRICK, Betty: As chief of the Lake Babine Nation in north central B.C., Betty Patrick co-authored the first book about the Lake Babine First Nation entitled *Cis Dideen Kat (When the Plumes Rise): The Way of the Lake Babine Nation* (2000) with Jo-Anne Fiske, a teacher of anthropology and women's studies at the University of Northern British Columbia. The book recalls the outlawed potlatch or "bibalhats" ceremonies and traces relations with the Canadian government and legal system. It also outlines their alternative traditional legal system with materials gleaned from interviews with elders and archival research.

PATRICK, Dorothy: Dorothy Patrick wrote the Carrier text for Sheila Thompson's bilingual *Cheryl Bibalhats/Cheryl's Potlatch* (1991), a children's book about a Carrier girl's naming ceremony in 1988 in Burns Lake. Patrick and Thompson also collaborated on *The Spirit of the Coast Salish* (1990), an educational text.

PIELLE, Sue: As an elder and storyteller of the Sliammon people, Sue Pielle joined with Anne Cameron, author of *Daughters of Copper Woman*, to present a West Coast traditional tale called *T'aal: The Woman Who Steals Bad Children* (1998). T'aal goes around after sunset with a basket made of writhing snakes, snatching up children who have defied their elders. When a young brother and sister are unfairly nabbed, they must free themselves and other children who have been captured. Pielle has worked with the Child Development Centre at Sliammon and in the Sliammon language and cultural program at James Thomson School.

SAM, Lillian: With the Nak'azdli Elders Society, Lillian Sam recorded the bilingual oral history of the Nak'azdli society in northern British Columbia in *Nak'azdli t'enne Yahulduk / Nak'azdli Elders Speak* (2001). Formerly known as the Necoslie, the Nak'azdli are members of the Dakelh (Carrier) people and are located near Fort St. James in northern British Columbia.

SAM, SR., Stanley: The history and stories of the Aboriginal people on Flores Island in Clayoquot Sound were told by Ahousaht elder Stanley Sam, Sr., in the *Ahousaht Wild Side Heritage Trail Guidebook* (1997), with a foreword by Robert Kennedy, Jr. Book sales supported the Ahousat Wild Side Heritage Trail Project to link the village of Ahousat with the beaches and headlands on the west side of Flores Island. Born in an Ahousat longhouse on February 29, 1928, Sam learned many stories from his grandfather partly because his poor health as a child kept him from attending residential school until age nine. For 54 years, he worked as a commercial fisherman. He also self-published *Tsasiits Himwica Disciplines: For A New Beginning of Life* (1999).

SANDY, Nancy: As an Aboriginal lawyer, Nancy Sandy prepared a section-by-section guide to the Indian Act for laypeople in *The Indian Act and What It Means* (1988).

Stanley Sam, Sr.

SELETZE, D. Johnnie: Born in 1920, Dolby Bevan Turner spent teenage years at Green Point on Cowichan Bay where she befriended members of the Khenipsen. In her eighties she profiled some of the elders she knew and relayed some of their stories in *When the Rains Came: And Other Legends of the Salish People* (1992), illustrated by Delmar Johnnie Seletze, a member of the Khenipsen band. Born in 1946, Seletze grew up in Duncan and studied art at Peninsula College of Art in Los Angeles and at Malaspina University-College.

SILVEY, Diane: Born in Egmont in 1946, Sechelt Band member Diane Silvey spent her early years in that small fishing village near the Skookumchuck Rapids. She graduated from UBC's Native Indian Teacher Education Program and taught for 21 years on reserves at Bella Bella and Port Alberni, and in Victoria. Her school text *From Time Immemorial: The First People of the Pacific Northwest Coast* (1999) was preceded by a children's book, *Spirit Quest* (1997), illustrated by her son Joe, and followed by *Raven's Flight* (2000), a young adult novel about a girl who gets into trouble on the streets of Vancouver. More recently Silvey provided the text for *The Kids Book of Aboriginal Peoples in Canada* (2005), illustrated by John Mantha, for ages eight to twelve.

Robert E. Stanley

STANLEY, Robert E: One of eleven siblings, Robert E. Stanley was born in the Nisga'a village of Gingolz, also known as Kincolith, on the northern coast of B.C., in 1958. His book *Northwest Native Arts: Basic Forms* (2002) shows how to draw the basic forms of Pacific Northwest First Nations art. His father Murphy Stanley, Sr., and his brothers Murphy, Jr., and Virgil are also artists.

VICKIE JENSEN PHOTO

Russell Stevens

STEVENS, Russell: Gitksan teacher and linguist Russell Stevens was born in Kispiox and died there in the late 1980s. He collaborated with Jay Powell in writing a set of language lessons for his eastern dialect of Gitksan: *Gitksan Language, Books 1 and 2* (1977). A virtuoso on the guitar and a natural teacher, he left his community with a continuing resource in the Gitksan people's efforts to maintain and revitalize their language and culture.

STUMP, Violet: The Alexandria band of approximately 70 Aboriginals on both banks of the Fraser River, about 75 kilometres north of Williams Lake, is the focus for *The People of Alexandria* (1990) by band chief Violet Stump and her sister **Sharon Stump**, illustrated by Maggie Ferguson-Dumais.

WILSON, Beatrice: Born in 1931, Haisla elder Beatrice Wilson was the granddaughter of Henaksiala chief Wakas (Solomon Robertson) and daughter of Nismulax (Gordon Robertson). She carries the name Li'inks of the Blackfish clan. She serves on the board of the Nanakila Institute and has been a leader in Haisla Rediscovery programs. She travels annually to the oolichan grounds in Kemano and harvests and preserves traditional foods in season. It is this cultural knowledge that she shared in

JAY POWELL PHOTO

Beatrice Wilson

Salmonberry Blossoms in the New Year (1995), by Alison Davis with Beatrice Wilson and Brian D. Compton.

WILSON, Solomon: Haida elder Solomon Wilson of Skidegate co-authored *The Knowledge and Use of Marine Invertebrates by the Skidegate Haida People of the Queen Charlotte Islands* (1981) with David W. Ellis.

WOLF, Annabel Cropped Eared: Born in 1951, Annabel Cropped Eared Wolf wrote *Shuswap History: A Century of Change* (1996), an introduction to the Shuswap First Nation. "Initially the Shuswap viewed the traders as friends and allies," she writes. "The Shuswap thought the fur trade would increase their material wealth and well-being and perhaps enhance their political status and power. As beaver were depleted, the fur trade declined. The Shuswap began to experience economic hardships and diseases. Their initial friendliness and peaceful co-existence with the traders were replaced in the middle of the 1820s with suspicion and resentment. The traders became victims of Indian threats, and the Shuswap refused to cooperate with the trade. In the 1840s economic conditions worsened and it was obvious that the traders wanted to dominate the Indians. . . . By the 1850s the Shuswap had lost much of their economic autonomy and were more under the power of the traders."

YELLOWHORN, Eldon: Born and raised on the Peigan Reserve in Alberta, Yellowhorn received his Ph.D. in anthropology from McGill. While teaching at SFU, he co-authored the revised version of Alan D. McMillan's *First Peoples in Canada* (2004).

V
CONTEXT

- Total B.C. Aboriginal population in 1996: **139,655**
- Percentage of overall B.C. population in 1996: **3.8**
- Total B.C. Aboriginal population in 2001: **170,000**
- Percentage of overall B.C. population in 2001: **4.4** (Increase indicates both a higher birth rate and an increasing willingness of citizens to identify themselves as Aboriginals to StatsCan.)

- Percentage of overall Aboriginal population of Canada that resided in B.C. in 2001: **17.5**
- Total B.C. Métis population included within Aboriginal population in 2001: **44,265**
- Percentage of B.C. Aboriginals now living off-reserve: **72**
- Aboriginal unemployment rate in B.C.: **21%**
- B.C.-wide unemployment rate: **6.9 %**

OFFICIAL ORGAN OF THE NATIVE BROTHERHOOD OF BRITISH COLUMBIA, INC.

VANCOUVER, B.C.   PRICE 10 CENTS

This "concentration camp" cartoon from the Native Voice *newspaper expresses the cynicism of returning World War II Aboriginal veterans. Aboriginal males in B.C. did not gain the right to vote provincially until **1949**. B.C. Aboriginals received the federal franchise in **1960**. They did not gain unrestricted access to purchase liquor until **1962**.*

NATIVE VOICE *CAPTION: "Our Editor—Ruth Smith has been editor of the* Native Voice *for 12 months out of the paper's 15 issues since inception in December, 1946. Mrs. Smith, a member of the Salish Indians, was born in Yale and educated at Coqualeetza residential school at Sardis. Mother of two children, her devotion to her duties as head of the only official native publication in Canada is an outstanding example to both native and white women the world over."*

• Average life expectancy in 1995 for a Canadian male (including Aboriginals): **75**
• Average life expectancy in 1995 for a male Aboriginal: **69**
• Average life expectancy in 1995 for a Canadian female (including Aboriginals): **82**

• Average life expectancy in 1995 for a female Aboriginal: **76**
• Percentage of Canadian Aboriginals in 1981 with university degrees: **2**
• Percentage of Non-Aboriginal population in 1981 with university degrees: **8.1**
• Percentage of Canadian Aboriginals in 1995 with university degrees: **4.2**
• Percentage of Non-Aboriginal population in 1995 with university degrees: **15.5**
• Year federal government created a $350 million healing fund and apologized to Aboriginal people of Canada "for past actions of the federal government which have contributed to the difficult pages in the history of our relationships together": **1998**

Canada's urban Aboriginal populations in 2001 (major cities)

Winnipeg	**55,760**
Edmonton	**40,930**
Vancouver	**36,855**
Calgary	**21,915**
Toronto	**20,300**
Saskatoon	**20,280**
Regina	**15,685**
Ottawa/Hull	**13,485**
Montreal	**11,085**

BC's urban Aboriginal populations in 2001 (excluding Vancouver)

Victoria	**8,695**
Prince George	**7,985**
Kamloops	**5,470**
Prince Rupert	**4,625**
Nanaimo	**4,335**
Abbotsford	**4,215**
Duncan	**4,085**
Chilliwack	**4,020**
Kelowna	**3,950**
Port Alberni	**3,340**
Williams Lake	**3,250**
Terrace	**3,085**
Vernon	**2,290**
Campbell River	**2,280**
Quesnel	**2,135**
Dawson Creek	**2,090**
Fort St. John	**1,785**
Courtenay	**1,735**
Cranbrook	**1,425**
Penticton	**1,290**
Powell River	**1,140**
Kitimat	**545**
Squamish	**545**
Parksville	**410**

━━━━━━━━━

• Number of treaties on Vancouver Island negotiated between First Nations and James Douglas between 1851 and 1854: **14**

• Decade when Lands commissioner Joseph Trutch denies Aboriginal rights, the need for treaties and and the rights of Aboriginals to pre-empt any Crown lands: **1860s**

Among the almost 30 residential schools in B.C., St. Mary's (above) was the oldest, founded as a school at Mission in the Fraser Valley in 1863. St. Mary's closed in 1985.

• Number of treaties lawfully concluded from Victoria during the next 140 years: **nil**
• Year that federal government prohibits Aboriginals from organizing to discuss land claims: **1927**
• Year that Native Brotherhood is secretly formed to discuss land claims: **1931**
• Year that lawyer Thomas Berger begins to argue (in the Frank Calder case) that Aboriginal title existed prior to Confederation: **1967**
• Year that the federal government initiates its preliminary negotiations with the Nisga'a First Nation: **1973**

• Year that B.C. government acknowledges the existence of Aboriginal rights and a new Claims Task Force recommends a six-step treaty negotiation process should be implemented: **1991**
• Year that Canada formally recognizes the inherent right to self-government as an existing Aboriginal right within the Canadian constitution: **1994**
• Year the Supreme Court of Canada issues Delgamuukw decision to confirm Aboriginal title includes the land itself, not only the right to hunt, fish and gather: **1997**

ABORIGINAL POPULATION OF BC:

1774: **250,000**
1835: **100,000**
1885:   **28,000**
1929:   **23,000**
1911:   **20,174**
1996: **139,655**
2001: **170,000**

'CHILDREN OF THE FIRST PEOPLE' JACKET DETAIL BY DOROTHY HAEGERT

GARY FIEGEHEN PHOTO [EBC]

Chief Joe Gosnell and Premier Glen Cark hold copies of the Nisga'a Treaty that they signed in 1998, before it was ratified as law in 2000.

• Year that Nisga'a, Canada and B.C. sign the Nisga'a Final Agreement to conclude treaty negotiations: **1998**

• Year that Nisga'a Agreement is ratified as law: **2000**

• Year that Nisga'a created their first Nisga'a Lands Committee: **1887**

• Number of treaties signed between B.C. First Nations and the B.C. government after the administration of Governor James Douglas to the premiership of Glen Clark: **1**

[Information herein was mainly derived from Robert J. Muckle's *The First Nations of British Columbia* (UBC Press, 1998), the BC Treaty Commission's *What's the deal with treaties?: A lay person's guide to treaty making in British Columbia* (2003), the *Encyclopedia of British Columbia* (Harbour, 2000), Alex Rose's *Spirit Dance at Meziadin* (Harbour, 2000), John W. Friesen & Virginia Lyons Friesen's *We Are Included: The Métis People of Canada Realize Riel's Vision* (Detselig, 2004), StatsCan and BC Stats.

"At this point in our struggle for survival, the Indian peoples of North America are entitled to declare a victory. We have survived. If others have also prospered on our land, let it stand as a sign between us that the Mother Earth can be good to all her children without confusing one with another. It is a myth of European warfare that one man's victory requires another's defeat."
—GEORGE MANUEL, THE FOURTH WAY (1974)

VICKIE JENSEN PHOTO

Gloria Cranmer Webster and Andrea Laforet of the Canadian Museum of Civilization unpack the repatriated Potlatch Collection for the new U'Mista Cultural Centre in 1980.

IV
BIBLIOGRAPHY

Adams, Howard. *The Education of Canadians.* Montreal: Harvest House, 1968.
————. *A History of the Métis of the Northwest.* Saskatoon: Modern Press, 1977.
————. *Prison of Grass: Canada from the Native Point of View.* Toronto: New Press, 1975.
————. *A Tortured People: The Politics of Colonization.* Penticton: Theytus, 1995.
Alfred, Agnes, Martine Reid & Daisy Sewid-Smith. *Paddling to Where I Stand: Agnes Alfred, Qwiqwasu'tinuxw Noblewoman.* Vancouver: UBC Press, 2004.
Alfred, Gerald Taiaiake. *Heeding the Voices of Our Ancestors: Kahnawake Mohawk Politics and the Rise of Native Nationalism.* Don Mills: Oxford U. Press, 1995.
————. *Peace, Power, Righteousness: An Indigenous Manifesto.* Don Mills: Oxford U. Press, 1999.
————. *Wasase: Indigenous Pathways of Action and Freedom.* Peterborough: Broadview Press, 2005.
Annharte. *Being on the Moon.* Winlaw: Polestar, 1990.
————. *Blueberry Canoe.* Vancouver: New Star, 2001.
————. *Coyote Columbus Café.* Winnipeg: Moonprint, 1994.
————. *Exercises in Lip Pointing.* Vancouver: New Star, 2003.
Antoine, Irene, et al. *Nak'al Bun Whudakelhne Bughuni: Stuart Lake, The People of their Words.* Vanderhoof: Yinka Déné Language Institute, 1991.
Archibald, Jo-Ann & Verna Kirkness. *The First Nations Longhouse: Our Home Away From Home.* Vancouver: First Nations House of Learning, 2001.
Arima, E.Y., Charles Jones, John Thomas, Denis St. Claire & Louis Clamhouse. *Between Ports Alberni and Renfrew: Notes on West Coast Peoples.* Mercury Series No. 46. Ottawa: Canadian Museum of Civilization, 1991.
Armstrong, Jeannette. *Breath Tracks.* Stratford: Williams-Wallace & Theytus, 1991.
————. *Dancing with the Cranes.* Penticton: Theytus, 2004.
————. *Enwhisteetkwa (Walk in Water).* Penticton: Okanagan Tribal Council, 1982.
————. *Looking at the Words of our People: First Nations Analysis of Literature.* Penticton: Theytus, 1993.
————. *Native Creative Process: A Collaborative Discourse Between Douglas Cardinal and Jeannette Armstrong.* Penticton: Theytus, 1991.
————. *Neekna and Chemai.* Penticton: Theytus, 1981.
————. *Slash.* Penticton: Theytus, 1983.
————. *Whispering in Shadows: A Novel.* Penticton: Theytus, 2000.
Armstrong, Jeannette, C. Armstrong & Lally Grauer, eds. *Native Poetry in Canada: A Contemporary Anthology.* Peterborough: Broadview Press, 2001.
Armstrong, Jeannette, Lee Maracle, Delphine Derickson & Greg Young-Ing, eds. *We Get Our Living Like Milk From The Land.* Penticton: The Okanagan Rights Committee, The Okanagan Indian Education Resource Society, 1993–94.
Arnott, Joanne. *Breasting the Waves: On Writing & Healing.* Vancouver: Press Gang, 1995.
————. *Ma MacDonald.* Toronto: Women's Press, 1993.
————. *My Grass Cradle.* Vancouver: Press Gang, 1992.
————. *Steepy Mountain Love Poetry.* Cape Croker: Kegedonce Press, 2004.
————. *Wiles of Girlhood.* Vancouver: Press Gang, 1991.
Assu, Harry & Joy Inglis. *Assu of Cape Mudge: Recollections of a Coastal Indian Chief.* Vancouver: UBC Press, 1989.
Atleo, Richard E. *Tsawalk: A Nuu-chah-nulth Worldview.* Vancouver: UBC Press, 2004.
Baker, Simon & Verna Kirkness. *Khot La Cha: The Autobiography of Chief Simon Baker.* Vancouver: Douglas & McIntyre, 1994.
Barbetti, Louise, et al. *We are our History – A Celebration of our Haisla Heritage.* Kitimat: Kitamaat Village Council, 2005.
Beynon, William. *Potlatch at Gitsegukla: William Beynon's 1945 Field Notebooks.* Eds. Margaret Seguin Anderson & Marjorie Halpin. Vancouver: UBC Press, 2000.
Bird, Catherine, et al. *The Boy Who Snared the Sun: A Carrier (Dakelh) Legend.* Ed. Rose Pierre. Illus. Roan Muntener. Vanderhoof: Yinka Déné Language Institute, 1994.

————. *Central Carrier Bilingual Dictionary.* Fort St. James: Carrier Linguistic Committee. 1974.

————. *The Robin and the Song Sparrow.* Ed. Rose Pierre. Illus. Roan Muntener. Vanderhoof: Yinka Déné Language Institute, 1994.

Blackstock, Michael. *Faces in the Forest: First Nations Art Created on Living Trees.* Montreal: McGill-Queen's U. Press, 2001.

————. *Salmon Run: A Florilegium of Aboriginal Ecological Poetry.* Kamloops: Wyget Books, 2005.

Borrows, John. *Aboriginal Law: Cases, Materials and Commentary.* Markham: Butterworths, 1998.

————. *The Resurgence of Indigenous Law.* Toronto: U. of Toronto Press, 2002.

Bose, Chris. *Somewhere in this Inferno.* Penticton: Theytus, 2004.

Boyd, Laura M. *'Atsoo and I.* Anahim Lake: Ulgatcho Indian Band, 1990.

————. *For Someone Special.* Quesnel: Nazko Indian Band, 1990.

————. *My Home Forever.* Quesnel: Nazko Indian Band, 1989.

Bruce, Skyros. *Kalala Poems.* Vancouver: Daylight Press, 1972.

Caffey, John & Ed Golstgrom, eds. *Shuswap History: The First 100 Years of Contact.* Kamloops: Secwepemc Cultural Education Society, 1990.

Campbell, Nicola I. *Shi-shi-etko.* Illus. Kim LaFave. Toronto: Groundwood, 2005.

Charleyboy, Orrey. *Tsi Del Del: Redstone.* Williams Lake: Chilcotin Language Committee, 1991.

Charlie, Domanic & August Jack Khahtsahlano. *Squamish Legends . . . The First People.* Ed. Oliver Wells. Vancouver: C. Chamberlain & F.T. Coan, 1966.

Chelsea, Phyllis, Vickie Jensen, Jay Powell & Celina Harry. *Learning Shuswap, Books 1–2.* Williams Lake: Alkali Lake Band, 1980.

Chrisjohn, Roland, Sherri Young & Michael Maraun. *The Circle Game: Shadows and Substance in the Indian Residential School Experience in Canada.* Penticton: Theytus, 1997.

Clements, Marie. *Burning Vision.* Vancouver: Talonbooks, 2003.

————. *The Girl Who Swam Forever.* Oxford: Miami U. Press, 2000.

————. *Now Look What You Made Me Do – Prerogatives.* Winnipeg: Blizzard, 1998.

————. *The Suitcase Chronicles.* Summerland: Journey Publication, 2002.

————. *The Unnatural and Accidental Women.* Vancouver: Talonbooks, 2005.

Clements, Marie, Greg Daniels & Margo Kane. *DraMétis: Three Métis Plays.* Penticton: Theytus, 2001.

Clutesi, George. *Potlatch.* Sidney: Gray's Publishing, 1969.

————. *Son of Raven, Son of Deer: Fables of the Tse-shaht People.* Sidney: Gray's Publishing, 1967.

————. *Stand Tall, My Son.* Illus. Mark Tebbett. Victoria: Newport Bay, 1990.

Cohen, Bill. *Stories and Images of What the Horse has Done for Us – An Illustrated History of Okanagan Ranching and Rodeo.* Penticton: Theytus, 1998.

Collins, Theo. *The Sechelt Act and What It Means.* Vancouver: Union of B.C. Indian Chiefs, 1988.

Cook, Margaret, Agnes Cranmer, J.V. Powell & Vickie Jenson. *Learning Kwak'wala.* Alert Bay: U'Mista Cultural Centre, 1980.

Courtoreille, Fred, Mary Armstrong & Terrance Armstrong. *Roast Moose & Rosaries: Fred & Mary's Story.* Moberly Lake: Two Sisters Publishing, 1997.

Cranmer, Agnes, Margaret Cook, J.V. Powell & Vickie Jenson. *Learning Kwak'wala.* Alert Bay: U'Mista Cultural Centre, 1980–1981.

Crey, Ernie & Suzanne Fournier. *Stolen From Our Embrace: The Abduction of First Nations Children and the Restoration of Aboriginal Communities.* Vancouver: Douglas & McIntyre, 1997.

Cuthand, Beth. *Horse Dance to Emerald Mountain.* Vancouver: Lazara Press, 1987.

————. *The Little Duck/Sikihpsis.* Illus. Mary Longman. Penticton: Theytus, 1999.

————. *Voices in the Waterfall*. Vancouver: Lazara Press, 1989.

Cuthand, Beth, co-ed. *Reinventing the Enemy's Language: Contemporary Native Women's Writings of North America*. New York: W.W. Norton, 1997.

Cuthand, Beth, ed. *Gatherings: The En'owkin Journal of First North American Peoples: Volume V*. Penticton: Theytus, 1994.

Davidson, Florence Edenshaw & Margaret Blackman. *During My Time: Florence Edenshaw Davidson, A Haida Woman*. Seattle: U. of Washington Press, 1982.

Dickson, Stewart & Raphael Ironstand (uncredited). *Hey Monias!: The Story of Raphael Ironstand*. Vancouver: Arsenal Pulp, 1993.

Dixon, Stan. *Self-Government, A Spirit Reborn*. Sechelt: Sechelt Indian Band, 1986.

Dove, Mourning. *Cogewea, The Half-Blood: A Depiction of the Great Montana Cattle Range*. Boston: Four Seas Co., 1927.

————. *Coyote Stories*. Lincoln: U. of Nebraska Press, 1990.

————. *Mourning Dove: A Salishan Autobiography*. Ed. Jay Miller. Lincoln: U. of Nebraska Press, 1990.

————. *Tales of the Okanogans*. Ed. Donald M. Hines. Fairfield: Ye Galleon Press, 1976.

Dumont, Marilyn. *Green Girl Dreams Mountains*. Lantzville: Oolichan, 2001.

————. *A Really Good Brown Girl*. London: Brick Books, 1996.

Einarson, Earl. *The Moccasins*. Illus. Julie Flett. Penticton: Theytus, 2004.

Eustache, Harold. *Shuswap Journey*. Penticton: Theytus, 2004.

Fife, Connie. *Beneath the Naked Sun*. Toronto: Sister Vision, 1992.

————. *Poems for a New World*. Vancouver: Ronsdale, 2001.

————. *Speaking Through Jagged Rock*. Fredericton: Broken Jaw Press, 1999.

Fife, Connie, ed. *The Colour of Resistance*. Toronto: Sister Vision, 1994.

Framst, Louise. *But I Cleaned My Room Last Year!* Cecil Lake: Framst Books, 2002.

————. *Feathers*. Cecil Lake: Framst Books, 2004.

————. *Kelly's Garden*. Cecil Lake: Framst Books, 1992.

————. *Manny's Many Questions*. Cecil Lake: Framst Books, 1992.

————. *On My Walk*. Cecil Lake: Framst Books, 2001.

————. *A Tahltan Cookbook, Vol. 1: Grace and George Edzerza Family*. Cecil Lake: Framst Books, 1995.

————. *A Tahltan Cookbook, Vol. 2: More than 88 Ways to Prepare Salmon*. Cecil Lake: Framst Books, 1996.

————. *A Tahltan Cookbook, Vol. 3: Campfire Cooking*. Cecil Lake: Framst Books, 1997.

Framst, Louise, ed. *A Community Tells Its Story: Cecil Lake 1925–2000*. Cecil Lake: Nor'Pioneer Women's Institute, 2000.

Galois, Robert, J.V. Powell & Gloria Cranmer Webster. *Kwakwaka'wakw Settlements, 1775–1920: A Geographical Analysis and Gazetteer*. Vancouver: UBC Press, 1994.

Gawa, Edith, Vickie Jensen & J.V. Powell, eds. *Gitxsanimax For Kids, Workbook 4*. Kispiox: Kispiox Band, 1977.

————. *Gitxsanimax For Kids, Workbook 5*. Kispiox: Kispiox Band, 1977.

George, Dan. *My Heart Soars*. Illus. Helmut Hirnschall. Saanichton: Hancock, 1974.

————. *My Spirit Soars*. Illus. Helmut Hirnschall. North Vancouver: Hancock, 1982.

————. *The Best of Chief Dan George*. Illus. Helmut Hirnschall. Surrey: Hancock, 2004.

George, Earl Maquinna. *Living On The Edge: Nuu-Chah-Nulth History from an Ahousaht Chief's Perspective*. Winlaw: Sono Nis, 2003.

George, Leonard. *Alternative Realities: The Paranormal, the Mystic, and the Transcendent in Human Experience*. New York: Facts on File, 1995.

————. *Crimes of Perception: An Encyclopedia of Heresies and Heretics*. New York: Paragon House, 1995.

Ghandl. *Nine Visits to the Mythworld: Ghandl of the Qayahl Llaanas*. Trans. Robert Bringhurst. Vancouver: Douglas & McIntyre, 2001.

Gottfriedson, Garry. *One Hundred Years of Contact*. Kamloops: Secwepemc Society, 1990.

————. *Glass Tepee*. Saskatoon: Thistledown, 2002.

————. *Painted Pony*. Illus. William McAusland. Kamloops: Partners in Publishing, 2005.

Gottfriedson, Garry & Reisa Smiley Schneider. *In Honour of Our Grandmothers: Imprints of Cultural Survival*. Illus. George Littlechild & others. Penticton: Theytus, 1994.

Guerin, Arnold. *Hunq'umi'num Language: Book 1*. Vancouver: Musqueam Band, 1993.

Hager, Barbara. *On Her Way: The Life and Music of Shania Twain*. New York: Berkley Boulevard, 1998.

————. *Honour Song: A Tribute*. Vancouver: Raincoast, 1996.

Hale, Janet Campbell. *Native Students with Problems of Addiction: A Manual for Adult Educators*. Salmon Arm: Native Adult Education Resource Centre, 1990.

Hall, Lizette. *The Carrier, My People*. Vanderhoof: Yinka Déné Institute, 2000.

Hamilton, Ron, et al. *Nuu-chah-nulth Phrase Book & Dictionary: Barkley Sound Dialect*. Bamfield: Barkley Sound Dialect Working Group, 2004.

Hanna, Darwin & Mamie Henry. *Our Tellings: Interior Salish Stories of the Nlha7kapmx People*. Vancouver: UBC Press, 1995.

Harris, Heather. *Rainbow Dancer*. Prince George: Caitlin, 1999.

Harris, Kenneth. *Visitors Who Never Left: The Origin of the People of Damelahamid*. Ed. Frances M.P. Robinson. Vancouver: UBC Press, 1974.

Harris, Martha Douglas. *History and Folklore of the Cowichan Indians*. Victoria: The Colonist Printing & Publishing Company, 1901.

Harry, Celina, Jay Powell, Vickie Jensen & Phyllis Chelsea. *Let's Study Shuswap, Books 1–2*. Williams Lake: Alkali Lake Band, 1977.

Harry, Celina, Jay Powell & Vickie Jensen. *Shuswap Teachers Manual*. Williams Lake: Alkali Lake Band, 1983.

Hart, Jim & Reg Davidson. *Haida Artifacts: An Exhibition with Commentaries*. Berkeley: Lowie Museum of Anthropology, U. of California, Lowe Art Museum, 1990.

Highway, Tomson. *Ernestine Shuswap Gets Her Trout*. Vancouver: Talonbooks, 2005.

Hungry Wolf, Beverly. *Daughters of the Buffalo Women: Maintaining the Tribal Faith*. Skookumchuck: Canadian Caboose Press, 1996.

————. *The Ways of my Grandmothers*. New York: William Morrow & Co., 1980.

Hunt, George & Franz Boas. *Kwakiutl Texts*. Leiden: E. J. Brill; New York: G. E. Stechert, 1905; New York: AMS Press, 1975.

————. *Kwakiutl Texts: Second Series*. Leiden: E. J. Brill; New York: G.E. Stechert, 1906; New York, AMS Press, 1975.

Hunter, Robert & Robert Calihoo. *Occupied Canada: A Young White Man Discovers His Unsuspected Past*. Toronto: McClelland & Stewart, 1991.

Jack, Agnes, ed. *Behind Closed Doors: Stories from the Kamloops Indian Residential School*. Penticton: Theytus, 2000.

Jacobson, Diane. *My Life in a Kwag'ul Big House*. Penticton: Theytus, 2005.

James, Rudy. *Devilfish Bay: The Giant Devilfish Story*. Woodinville: Wolfhouse Pub., 1997.

Jensen, Doreen & Polly Sargent. *Robes of Power: Totem Poles on Cloth*. Vancouver: UBC Press, 1987.

Jensen, Doreen. *In Celebration of our Survival: The First Nations of British Columbia*. Vancouver: UBC Press, 1991.

John, Gracie & Marie John, Jr. *Saik'us Whut'enne Hubughunek*. Vanderhoof: Yinka Déné Language Institute, 1991.

John, Mary & Bridget Moran. *Stoney Creek Woman: The Story of Mary John*. Vancouver: Pulp Press & Tillacum Library, 1989.

John, Peter & Doris Johnson. *Highu Yalht'uk / Elders Speak: The Story of Peter John*. Burns Lake: School District #55, 2000.

Johnson, E. Pauline. *Canadian Born*. Toronto: Morang, 1903.

————. *Flint and Feather*. Toronto: Musson, 1912; *Flint and Feather: The Complete Poems of E. Pauline Johnson*. Hodder & Stoughton, 1917.

―――. *Legends of Vancouver.* Vancouver: privately printed in 1911 by the Pauline Johnson Trust Fund from the *Province Magazine,* followed by many editions, including Vancouver: G.S. Forsyth, 1913.

―――. *The Moccasin Maker.* Toronto: William Briggs, 1913.

―――. *North American Indian Silver Craft.* Vancouver: Subway Books, 2005.

―――. *"When George was King" and Other Poems.* Brockville: Brockville Times, 1908.

―――. *The White Wampum.* London: John Lane; Boston: Lamson, Wolffe; Toronto: Copp Clark, 1895.

―――. *The Shagganappi.* Toronto: William Briggs, 1913.

Johnson, Mary, Jay Powell, Vickie Jensen & Edith Gawa. *Gitxsanimax for Kids, Books 1–7.* Kispiox: Kispiox Indian Band, 1977–1980.

Jones, Charles & Stephen Busustow. *Queesto: Pacheenaht Chief by Birthright.* Nanaimo: Theytus, 1981.

Joseph, Gene. *Sharing the Knowledge: A First Nations Resource Guide.* Vancouver: United Native Nations, Legal Services Society, 1992.

Kew, Della & P.E. Goddard. *Indian Art and Culture of the Northwest Coast.* Saanichton: Hancock House, 1974.

Khahtsahlano, August Jack & Major J.S. Matthews. *Conversations with Khatsahlano 1932–1954.* Vancouver City Archives, 1969.

Kirkness, Verna J. *Indians of the Plains.* Toronto: Grolier, 1985.

―――. *Aboriginal Languages: A Collection of Talks and Papers.* Vancouver: V.J. Kirkness, 1998.

Kirkness, Verna J. & Sheena Selkirk Bowman. *First Nations and Schools: Triumphs and Struggles.* Toronto: Canadian Education Association, 1992.

Koon, Danny. Untitled art book. Alert Bay, 1971.

Large, R. Geddes & Charlie George (uncredited). *Soogwilis: A Collection of Kwakiutl Indian Designs & Legends.* Toronto: Ryerson Press, 1951.

Larson, Walt. *From the Wilderness.* Westminster: Karmichael Press, 1996.

Lawrence, Mary. *In Spirit & Song.* Coburg: Highway Bookshop, 1992.

―――. *My People, Myself.* Prince George: Caitlin, 1997.

Louis, Shirley. *Q'sapi: A History of Okanagan People as told by Okanagan Families.* Penticton: Theytus, 2002.

Loyie, Larry & Constance Brissenden. *As Long as the Rivers Flow: A Last Summer Before Residential School.* Illus. Heather D. Holmlund. Toronto: Groundwood, 2003.

―――. *The Gathering Tree.* Illus. Heather D. Holmlund. Penticton: Theytus, 2005.

Loyie, Larry & Vera Manuel. *Two Plays About Residential School.* Vancouver: Living Traditions, 1998.

Loyie, Larry, co-ed. *The Wind Cannot Read: An Anthology of Learners Writing.* Victoria: Province of British Columbia Ministry of Advanced Education, Training & Technology, 1992.

Mack, Clayton & Harvey Thommasen. *Bella Coola Man: More Stories of Clayton Mack.* Madeira Park: Harbour, 1994.

―――. *Grizzlies & White Guys: The Stories of Clayton Mack.* Madeira Park: Harbour, 1993.

MacLeod, Heather Simeney. *The Burden of Snow.* Winnipeg: Turnstone, 2004.

―――. *My Flesh, the Sound of Rain.* Regina: Coteau, 1998.

―――. *Shapes of Orion.* Smoking Lung Press, 2000.

MacLeod, Heather Simeney & Coral Hull. *The North Woods.* New York: Rattapallax Press, 2003.

Malloway, Richard. *The Chilliwack Story of the Sxwayxwey.* Recorded & transcribed by Dr. Norman Todd. Sardis: Coqualeetza Cultural Centre, circa 1986.

Malloway, Richard & Brian Thom. *Telling Stories: The Life of Chief Richard Malloway.* Stó:lo Tribal Council, 1994.

Manuel, George & Michael Posluns. *The Fourth Way: An Indian Reality.* Toronto: Collier-Macmillan, 1974.

Maracle, Lee. *Bent Box.* Penticton: Theytus, 2000.

————. *Bobbi Lee, Indian Rebel.* Toronto: Women's Press, 1975.

————. *Daughters are Forever.* Vancouver: Raincoast, 2002.

————. *I Am Woman.* Vancouver: Write-On Press, 1988.

————. *I Am Woman: A Native Perspective on Sociology and Feminism.* Vancouver: Press Gang, 1996.

————. *Ravensong.* Vancouver: Press Gang, 1993.

————. *Sojourner's Truth.* Vancouver: Press Gang, 1992.

————. *Sojourners & Sundogs.* Vancouver: Press Gang, 1999.

————. *Sundogs.* Penticton: Theytus, 1992.

————. *Will's Garden.* Penticton: Theytus, 2002.

Maracle, Lee & Leanne Flett Kruger. *Gatherings: The En'owkin Journal of First North American Peoples: Volume XIII.* Penticton: Theytus, 2002.

Maracle, Lee & Sandra Laronde, eds. *My Home As I Remember.* Toronto: National Cultural Heritage Foundation, 1998.

Maracle, Lee, et al. *Telling It: Women and Language Across Cultures.* Vancouver: Press Gang, 1994.

Marchand, Len & Matt Hughes. *Breaking Trail.* Prince George: Caitlin, 2000.

Marsden, Solomon (Gitksan language editor), Abel Campbell & Edith Campbell. *Learning Gitksan, Book 3, Western Dialect.* Kitwancool: Kitwancool, Kitsegukla & Kitwanga Indian Bands, 1980.

Marsden, Solomon (Gitksan language editor), J.V. Powell & Vickie Jensen. *Learning Gitksan, Book 2, Western Dialect.* Kitwancool: Kitwancool, Kitsegukla & Kitwanga Indian Bands, 1980.

————. *Learning Gitksan, Book 4, Western Dialect.* Kitwancool: Kitwancool, Kitsegukla & Kitwanga Indian Bands, 1980.

McIvor, Dorothy Matheson. *Coqualeetza: "Vestiga Nulla Retrosum" (No Backward Step).* Surrey: Blue Pine Publishing, 1978.

Michell, Teresa. *How the Coho Got his Hooked Nose.* Sardis: Coqualeetza Education Training Centre, 1981.

————. *The Mischievous Cubs.* Sardis: Coqualeetza Education Training Centre, 1981.

Morisset, Jean & Rose-Marie Pelletier, eds. *Ted Trindell: Métis Witness to the North.* Vancouver: Pulp Press & Tillacum Library, 1987.

Mortimer, Hilda with Chief Dan George. *You Call Me Chief: Impressions of the Life of Chief Dan George.* Toronto: Doubleday, 1981.

Nahanee, Gloria & Kay Johnston. *Spirit of Powwow.* Surrey: Hancock, 2003.

Napoleon, Art. *Native Studies of North Eastern B.C.* Salmon Arm: Native Adult Education Resource Centre, 1991.

Neel, David. *Our Chiefs and Elders: Words and Photographs of Native Leaders.* Vancouver: UBC Press, 1992.

————. *The Great Canoes: Reviving a Northwest Coast Tradition.* Vancouver: Douglas & McIntyre, 1995.

Nowell, Charles James & Clelland Stearns Ford. *Smoke from Their Fires: The Life of a Kwakiutl Chief.* New Haven: Yale U. Press, 1941.

Nuytten, Phil. *The Totem Carvers: Charlie James, Ellen Neel, and Mungo Martin.* Vancouver: Panorama Publications, 1982.

O'Connor, Joseph, Natasha Netschay Davies & Lloyd Dolha. *Smoke Signals from the Heart.* Vancouver: Totem Pole Books, 2004.

Odjig, Daphne. *Odjig: The Art of Daphne Odjig, 1985–2000.* Toronto: Key Porter, 2000.

————. *Tales of the Nanabush: Books of Indian Legends for Children.* 10 Vols. Toronto, 1971.

Odjig, Daphne, R.M. Vanderburgh & M.E. Southcott. *A Paintbrush in my Hand.* Toronto: Natural Heritage, 1993.

Patrick, Betty & Jo-Anne Fiske. *Cis Dideen Kat (When the Plumes Rise): The Way of the Lake Babine Nation.* Vancouver: UBC Press, 2000.

Paul, Philip Kevin. *Taking the Names Down from the Hill.* Roberts Creek: Nightwood, 2003.

Pennier, Henry. *Chiefly Indian: The Warm and Witty Story of a British Columbia Half-Breed Logger.* Ed. Herbert L. McDonald. Vancouver: Gray-Donald Graphics, 1972.

Pielle, Sue with Anne Cameron. *T'AAL: The One Who Takes Bad Children.* Madeira Park: Harbour, 1998.

Pierce, William H. *From Potlatch to Pulpit, Being the Autobiography of Rev. William Henry Pierce, Native Missionary To the Indian Tribes of the Northwest Coast of British Columbia.* Ed. J.P. Hicks. Vancouver: The Vancouver Bindery, 1933.

Point, Susan. *Susan Point: Coast Salish Artist.* Ed. Gary Wyatt. Vancouver: Douglas & McIntyre, 2000.

Prince, Louis-Billy. *The Little Dwarves and the Creation of Nak'azdli: A Carrier Legend.* Transcribed by Father Adrien-Gabriel Morice. Vanderhoof: Yinka Déné Language Institute, 1996.

Reid, Bill. *All the Gallant Beasts and Monsters.* Vancouver: Buschlen-Mowatt, 1992.

————. *Solitary Raven: The Selected Writings of Bill Reid.* Vancouver: Douglas & McIntyre, 2001.

Reid, Bill & Adelaide de Menil. *Out of the Silence.* New York: Harper & Row, 1971.

Reid, Bill & Bill Holm. *Form and Freedom: A Dialogue on Northwest Coast Indian Art.* Houston: Rice U. Institute for the Arts, 1975.

Reid, Bill & Robert Bringhurst. *The Raven Steals the Light.* Vancouver: Douglas & McIntyre, 1984.

Robinson, Eden. *Blood Sports.* Toronto: McClelland & Stewart, 2006.

————. *Monkey Beach.* Toronto: Knopf, 2000.

————. *Traplines.* Toronto: Knopf, 1996.

Robinson, Gordon. *Tales of Kitamaat.* Illus. Vincent Haddelsey. Kitimat: Northern Sentinel Press, 1956.

Robinson, Harry. *Living by Stories: A Journey of Landscape and Memory.* Ed. Wendy Wickwire. Vancouver: Talonbooks, 2005.

————. *Nature Power: In the Spirit of an Okanagan Storyteller.* Ed. Wendy Wickwire. Vancouver: Douglas & McIntyre, 1992.

————. *Write It On Your Heart: The Epic World of an Okanagan Storyteller.* Ed. Wendy Wickwire. Vancouver: Theytus & Talonbooks, 1989.

Rosetti, Bernadette. *Kw'eh Ts'u Haindene: Descendants of Kwah – A Carrier Indian Genealogy.* Fort St. James: Carrier Linguistic Committee & Necoslie Indian Band, 1979.

————. *Musdzi 'Udada'/The Owl Story: A Carrier Indian Legend.* Vanderhoof: Yinka Déné Language Institute, 1991.

————. *Nunulk'i'-un.* Fort St. James: Carrier Linguistic Committee, n.d.

Sam, Lillian, ed. *Nak'azdli t'enne Yahulduk / Nak'azdli Elders Speak .* Penticton: Theytus, 2001.

Sam, Sr., Stanley M. *Ahousaht Wild Side Heritage Trail Guidebook.* Illus. Eddie Sam. Vancouver: Western Canada Wilderness Committee, 1997.

————. *Tsasiits Himwica Disciplines: For A New Beginning of Life.* Ahousaht: Fleming Printing, Victoria, 1999.

Sandy, Nancy. *The Indian Act and What It Means.* Union of B.C. Indian Chiefs, 1988.

Schwarz, Herbert T. *Windigo And Other Tales of the Ojibways.* Illus. Norval Morrisseau. Toronto: McClelland & Stewart, 1969.

Scofield, Gregory. *The Gathering: Stones for the Medicine Wheel.* Vancouver: Polestar, 1994.

————. *I Knew Two Métis Women: The Lives of Dorothy Scofield and Georgiana Houle Young.* Victoria: Polestar, 1999.

————. *Love Medicine and One Song.* Victoria: Polestar 1997.

252

————. *Native Canadiana: Songs from the Urban Rez.* Vancouver: Polestar, 1996.

————. *Singing Home the Bones.* Vancouver: Polestar, 2005.

————.*Thunder Through My Veins: Memories of a Métis Childhood.* Toronto: HarperFlamingo, 1998.

Sealey, D. Bruce & Verna J. Kirkness, eds. *Indians Without Tipis: A Resource Book by Indians and Métis.* Winnipeg: William Clare, 1973.

Seaweed, Willie. *Innovations for a Changing Time: Willie Seaweed, A Master Kwakiutl Artist.* Seattle: Pacific Science Center, 1992.

Seaweed, Willie & Bill Holm. *Smoky-Top, The Art and Times of Willie Seaweed.* Thomas Burke Memorial Washington State Museum monograph. Seattle: U. of Washington Press, 1983.

Sepass, Khalserten. *The Songs of the Y-Ail-Mihth.* Vancouver: 1958.

————. *Sepass Poems.* Ed. Eloise Street. Trans. C.L. Street. Preface by Chief Waupauka LaHurreau. Vancouver, 1955; *Sepass Poems: Songs of Y-Ail-Mihth.* New York: Vantage, 1963; *Sepass Tales: Songs of Y-Ail-Mihth.* Chilliwack: Sepass Trust, 1974.

Sewid, James P. *Guests Never Leave Hungry: The Autobiography of James Sewid, a Kwakiutl Indian.* Ed. James P. Spradley. New Haven: Yale U. Press, 1969.

Sewid-Smith, Daisy. *Prosecution or Persecution.* Cape Mudge: Nu-Yum-Baleess Society, 1979.

Sewid-Smith, Daisy & Martine Jeanne Reid. *Paddling to Where I Stand: Agnes Alfred, Qwiqwasu'tinuxw Noblewoman.* Vancouver: UBC Press, 2004.

Silvey, Diane. *From Time Immemorial: The First People of the Pacific Northwest Coast.* Gabriola: Pacific Edge Publishing, 1999.

————. *The Kids Book of Aboriginal Peoples in Canada.* Illus. John Mantha. Toronto: Kids Can Press, 2005.

————. *Raven's Flight.* Vancouver: Raincoast, 2000.

————. *Spirit Quest.* Vancouver: Beach Holme, 1997.

Sinclair, Lister & Jack Pollock, eds. *The Art of Norval Morrisseau.* Toronto: Methuen; New York: Routledge & Kegan Paul, 1979.

SKAAY. *Being in Being: The Collected Works of SKAAY of the Qquuna Qiighawaay.* Trans. Robert Bringhurst. Vancouver: Douglas & McIntyre, 2001.

Smith, M. Jane. *Returning the Feathers: Five Gitxsan Stories.* Illus. Ken Mowatt. Smithers: Creekstone & Sandhill, 2004.

Speck, Henry. *Kwakiutl Art: Its Background and Traditions.* Vancouver: Indian Designs Ltd., 1963.

Stanley, Robert E. *Northwest Native Arts: Basic Forms.* Surrey: Hancock, 2002.

Sterling, Shirley. *My Name is Seepeetza.* Toronto: Groundwood, 1992.

Stevens, Russell & Jay Powell. *Gitksan Language, Books 1 and 2.* Kispiox: Kispiox Band, 1977.

Stump, Sarain. *There Is My People Sleeping: The Ethnic Poem-Drawings of Sarain Stump.* Sidney: Gray's Publishing, 1970.

Stump, Violet & Sharon Stump. *The People of Alexandria.* Illus. Maggie Ferguson-Dumais. Developing Our Resources Curriculum Project, Quesnel Native Education Program, 1990.

Swan, Luke Francis & David Ellis. *Teachings of the Tides: Uses of Marine Invertebrates by the Manhousat People.* Nanaimo: Theytus, 1981.

Tappage, Mary Augusta. *The Big Tree and the Little Tree.* Illus. Terry Gallagher. Winnipeg: Pemmican, 1986.

————. *Days of Augusta.* Ed. Jean E. Speare. Photos by Robert Keziere. Vancouver: J.J. Douglas, 1973.

Tate, Henry W. *The Porcupine Hunter and Other Stories: The Original Tsimshian Texts of Henry W. Tate.* Ed. Ralph Maud. Vancouver: Talonbooks, 1993.

Tate, Henry W. & Franz Boas. *Tsimshian Mythology: Based On Texts Recorded By Henry W. Tate.* Washington D.C.: 31st Annual Report of the U.S. Bureau of American Ethnology 1909–1910, 1916.

Thompson, Sheila. *Cheryl Bibalhats/Cheryl's Potlatch.* Vanderhoof: Yinka Déné Language Institute, 1991.

————. *The Spirit of the Coast Salish.* North Vancouver: Creative Curriculum Inc., 1990.

Turner, Dolby. *When the Rains Came: And Other Legends of the Salish People.* Illus. D. Jonnie Seletze. Victoria: Orca, 1992.

Van Camp, Richard. *Angel Wing Splash Pattern.* Wiarton: Kegedonce Press, 2002.

————. *The Lesser Blessed.* Vancouver: Douglas & McIntyre, 1996.

————. *A Man Called Raven.* Illus. George Littlechild. San Francisco: Children's Book Press, 1997.

————. *What's the Most Beautiful Thing You Know About Horses?* Illus. George Littlechild. San Francisco: Children's Book Press, 1988.

Vickers, Roy Henry. *Copperman: The Art of Roy Henry Vickers.* Tofino: Eagle Dancer, 2003.

————. *Spirit Transformed: A Journey from Tree to Totem.* Photography by Bob Herger. Vancouver: Raincoast, 1996.

————. *Solstice: The Art of Roy Vickers.* Tofino: Eagle Dancer & Raincoast, 1988.

Vickers, Roy Henry & Dave Bouchard. *The Elders Are Watching.* Tofino: Eagle Dancer, 1990.

Walkus, Sr., Simon. *Oowekeeno Oral Traditions as Told by the Late Chief Simon Walkus, Sr.* Eds. John Rath & Susanne Hilton. Trans. Eveyln Walkus Windsor. Mercury Series #84. Ottawa: National Museum of Man, 1982.

Wallas, James & Pamela Whitaker. *Kwakiutl Legends.* North Vancouver: Hancock, 1981.

Walsh, Anthony & Children of the Inkameep Day School. *The Tale of the Nativity.* Illus. Francis Batiste. Victoria: Committee for the Revival & Furtherance of B.C. Indian Arts, 1940.

Webster, Gloria Cranmer. *The Kwakwaka'wakw and the Spirit Lodge.* Vancouver: Expo 86, 1986.

Webster, Peter S. *As Far As I Know: Reminiscences of an Ahousat Elder.* Illus. Kwayatsapalth. Campbell River: Campbell River Museum & Archives, 1983.

Wheeler, Jordan. *Chuck in the City.* Illus. Bill Cohen. Penticton: Theytus, 2000.

White, Ellen. *Kwulasulwut: Stories From the Coast Salish.* Illus. David Neel. Nanaimo: Theytus, 1981.

————. *Kwulasulwut II: More Salish Creation Stories.* Illus. Bill Cohen. Penticton: Theytus, 1997.

William, Gerry. *The Black Ship: Book One of Enid Blue Starbreaks.* Penticton: Theytus, 1994.

————. *The Woman in the Trees.* Vancouver: New Star, 2004.

Williams, Gloria C. & Maria Bolanz. *Tlingit Art: Totem Poles & Art of the Alaskan Indians.* Surrey: Hancock, 2003.

Williams, Lorna. *Exploring Mount Currie.* Vancouver: Douglas & McIntyre, 1982.

————. *Sima7: Come Join Me.* Vancouver: Pacific Educational Press, 1991.

Wilson, Ardythe (Skanu'u). *Heartbeat of the Earth: A First Nations Artist Records Injustice and Resistance.* Gabriola: New Society Publishers, 1996.

Wilson, Ardythe (Skanu'u) & Don Monet. *Colonialism on Trial: Indigenous Land Rights and the Gitksan Wet'suwet'en Sovereignty Case.* Gabriola: New Society Publishers, 1991.

Wilson, Beatrice & Alison Davis. *Salmonberry Blossoms in the New Year: Some Culturally Significant Plants of the Haisla known to occur within the Greater Kitlope Ecosystem.* Kitimat: Nanakila Press, 1995.

Wilson, Solomon & David Ellis. *The Knowledge and Use of Marine Invertebrates by the Skidegate Haida People of the Queen Charlotte Islands.* Skidegate: Queen Charlotte Islands Museum Society, 1981.

Wolf, Annabel Cropped Eared. *Shuswap History: A Century of Change.* Kamloops: Secwepemc Cultural Education Society, 1996.

Wright, Marion. *My Elders Tell Me.* Port Hardy: Tri-Bands Education Committee, 1996.

Wright, Walter. *Men of Medeek.* Kitimat: Northern Sentinel Press, 1962.

Yahgulanaas, Michael Nicoll. *Last Voyage of the Black Ship*. Vancouver: Western Canada
    Wilderness Committee, 2002.
————. *A Lousy Tale*. Self-published, 2004.
————. *A Tale of Two Shamans*. Penticton: Theytus, 2001.
Yellowhorn, Eldon & Alan D. McMillan. *First Peoples in Canada*. Vancouver: Douglas &
    McIntyre, 2004.
York, Annie Zetco & Andrea Laforet. *Spuzzum: Fraser Canyon Histories, 1808–1939*.
    Vancouver: UBC Press & Canadian Museum of Civilization, 1998.
York, Annie, Richard Daly, & Chris Arnett. *They Write Their Dreams on the Rock Forever:
    Rock writings in the Stein River Valley of British Columbia*. Vancouver: Talonbooks,
    1993.
Young-Ing, Greg. *The Random Flow of Blood and Flowers*. Victoria: Ekstasis, 1996.

Young-Ing, Greg, ed. *IndigeCrit: Aboriginal
    Perspectives on Aboriginal Literature*.
    Vancouver: Theytus, 2001.
————. *Gatherings: The En'owkin Journal of First
    North American Peoples: Volume II*.
    Penticton: Theytus, 1991.
————. *Gatherings: The En'owkin Journal of First
    North American Peoples: Volume III*.
    Penticton: Theytus, 1993.
————. *Gatherings: The En'owkin Journal of First
    North American Peoples: Volume IX*.
    Penticton: Theytus, 1998.
Young-Ing, Greg & Florene Belmore, eds.
    *Gatherings: The En'owkin Journal of First
    North American Peoples: Volume X*.
    Penticton: Theytus, 1999.

*Randy Fred, Theytus Books founder,
received the Gray Campbell
Distinguished Service Award (2005).*

Theytus publisher Anita Large (2004)

255

VII
INDEX OF ENTRIES

BARRY PETERSON & BLAISE ENRIGHT-PETERSON PHOTO

Alan Twigg has produced the cultural
newspaper *BC BookWorld* since 1987, as well as
six documentary films. In recent years he has
compiled a public service reference site,
hosted by Simon Fraser University, that
provides information on more than 7,000
British Columbia authors. He also provides
the administration for several book prizes
and teaches a course on the history of
British Columbia literature for SFU.
He lives with his family in Vancouver.

ALSO AVAILABLE:

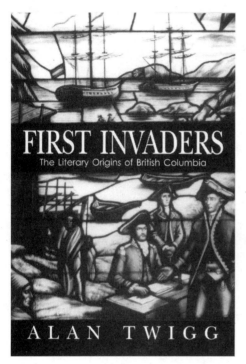

"I got lost and found in it."
— EDITH IGLAUER,
AUTHOR OF FISHING WITH JOHN

"the most enjoyable book
on B.C. history that I have
read for years."
— JIM CHRISTY, GEORGIA STRAIGHT

"Engrossing..."
— DAVID COLTERJOHN, VANCOUVER SUN

"Fascinating... Studded with
scads of maps and illustrations..."
— LYNNE VAN LUVEN, TIMES COLONIST

"There is absolutely no
substitute for this panorama of
our shared beginnings."
—MARK FORSYTHE, CBC ALMANAC

First Invaders is the first overview of the earliest literary works
pertaining to British Columbia, complete with maps, illustrations
and original photos. *First Invaders* recalls the drama and confusion
arising from the initial contacts between Europeans, Americans
and the First Nations on Canada's West Coast.

*Nominated for a 2005 BC Book Prize
(Hubert Evans Non-Fiction Award)*
•
*Honourable Mention:
BC Historical Federation Awards*

Published by Ronsdale • www.ronsdalepress.com
$21.95 CDN; $18.95 USA; ISBN: 1-55380-018-4